Huánuco Pampa

NEW ASPECTS OF ANTIQUITY

General Editor: COLIN RENFREW

Consulting Editor for the Americas: JEREMY A. SABLOFF

CRAIG MORRIS and DONALD E. THOMPSON

Huánuco Pampa
An Inca City and its Hinterland

with 126 illustrations, 14 in colour

THAMES AND HUDSON

To Donald Collier

who first instilled in both of us
a passion for the Andes

© 1985 Thames and Hudson Ltd, London

Printed and bound in Hungary

Contents

Foreword from the Editors

When the Conquistadors overwhelmed the Inca world in 1532, a whole human way of life vanished, never to return. Historians have often turned to the written sources for the period of this cataclysm and its immediate aftermath. And archaeologists have frequently drawn upon the documentary materials dating from the time of the spread of European influence in the New World in seeking to interpret their data. But it is probably fair to say that the information from the written documents and the findings of modern archaeology have rarely been brought together very successfully.

In this remarkable study of an administrative outpost within the Inca empire, Craig Morris and Donald Thompson demonstrate how effectively a careful analysis of the written records which survive can be brought to bear upon new archaeological data, and how those data can give new weight and emphasis to the documentation. They show how their integrated approach can rectify long-standing misconceptions which have been based on superficial readings of limited historical sources. In particular, they are able convincingly to argue that older studies of the Inca empire have been wrong in focussing almost exclusively upon Cuzco, the capital city of the Incas, and have failed to recognize the importance of the secondary administrative centers, of which Huánuco Pampa was one. The empire looks very different when it is seen, not just from the capital looking outwards, but from the hinterland looking towards the center.

The authors also provide new information on the functioning of complex pre-industrial societies, which indicates that the major institutions within Inca society, notably the economic and political organizations, were not so clearly separated nor so well defined as was the case in several other early state societies. They show too that trading activity and market exchange, which have received considerable attention from archaeologists in recent years, appear relatively underdeveloped among the Inca, when their civilization is compared with other state societies.

Above all, Craig Morris and Donald Thompson have succeeded in giving a graphic picture of life in one corner of the Inca empire, drawing upon the results both of their own fieldwork, and their careful analysis of the various surviving documents from the immediately post-Conquest period. Students of

South American archaeology will find here much that is new and original, while those less familiar with the Inca world will glimpse something not only of the human reality behind the artifacts, but of the life and pleasure of archaeologists in the field.

The Inca state as a whole is seen more clearly in this study of Huánuco Pampa, one of its provincial capitals, and its accompanying territory. With their interdisciplinary approach, and through their energy in the field, the authors have succeeded in rescuing one more part of that vanished world from oblivion.

Jeremy A. Sabloff

Colin Renfrew

1 An empire destroyed and rediscovered

On the evening of Saturday, 16 November 1532, the Inca, Atahualpa, approached the city of Cajamarca, in what is now Peru, where the Spaniards under Francisco Pizarro awaited him in ambush. The 19th-century historian William Prescott, drawing upon a selection of eyewitness Spanish accounts, vividly describes the events which followed:[1]

It was not long before sunset, when the van of the royal procession entered the gates of the city. First came some hundreds of the menials, employed to clear the path from every obstacle, and singing songs of triumph as they came. . . . Then followed other bodies of different ranks, and dressed in different liveries. Some wore a showy stuff, checkered white and red, like the squares of a chess-board. Others were clad in pure white, bearing hammers or maces of silver or copper; and the guards, together with those in immediate attendance on the prince, were distinguished by rich azure livery, and a profusion of gay ornaments, while the large pendants attached to the ears indicated the Peruvian noble.

plates VI, 10

Elevated high above his vassals came the Inca Atahuallpa, borne on a sedan or open litter, on which was a sort of throne made of massive gold of inestimable value. The palanquin was lined with the richly colored plumes of tropical birds, and studded with shining plates of gold and silver. The monarch's attire was much richer than on the preceding evening. Round his neck was suspended a collar of emeralds of uncommon size and brilliancy. His short hair was decorated with golden ornaments, and the imperial *borla* encircled his temples. The bearing of the Inca was sedate and dignified; and from his lofty station he looked down on the multitudes below with an air of composure, like one accustomed to command.

As the leading files of the procession entered the great square, larger, says an old chronicler, than any square in Spain, they opened to the right and left for the royal retinue to pass. Everything was conducted with admirable order. The monarch was permitted to traverse the *plaza* in silence, and not a Spaniard was to be seen. When some five or six thousand of his people had entered the place, Atahuallpa halted, and, turning round with an inquiring look, demanded, 'Where are the strangers?'

At this moment Fray Vicente de Valverde, a Dominican friar, Pizarro's chaplain, and afterward Bishop of Cuzco, came forward with his breviary, or, as other accounts say, a Bible, in one hand, and a crucifix in the other, and, approaching the Inca, told him, that he came, by order of his commander to expound to him the doctrines of the true faith, for which purpose the Spaniards had come from a great distance to his country. . . .

Whether Atahuallpa possessed himself of every link in the curious chain of argument by which the monk connected Pizarro with St. Peter, may be doubted. It is certain, however, that he must have had very incorrect notions of the Trinity, if, as Garcilasso states, the interpreter Felipillo explained it by saying, that 'the Christians believed in three Gods and one God, and that made four.' But there is no doubt he perfectly comprehended that the drift of the discourse was to persuade him to resign his sceptre and acknowledge the supremacy of another.

He then demanded of Valverde by what authority he had said these things. The friar pointed to the book which he held, as his authority. Atahuallpa, taking it, turned over the pages a moment, then, as the insult he had received probably flashed across his mind, he threw it down with vehemence, and exclaimed, – 'Tell your comrades that they shall give me an account of their doings in my land. I will not go from here, till they have made me full satisfaction for all the wrongs they have committed.'

This re-creation based on Prescott's reading of the Spanish sources available to him helps give life to Inca culture in the fateful moment that its destruction was assured. It was a culture with a rich court life and an aesthetic which is only partly preserved in the monuments and artifacts that escaped destruction. The conflict which would lead to the downfall of the Inca and his state was already set in motion by the time the scene between Atahualpa and the priest transpired. Beyond his unwillingness to accept a foreign god the Inca ruler failed to guess the military practices of the Spaniards and the risks to which he had allowed himself to be subjected. The Spaniards had persuaded Atahualpa that his people should enter the city unarmed, while hiding their own forces in the large buildings that apparently surrounded Cajamarca's plaza. What we see in Atahualpa is not so much a naive military strategist, but a ruler from a completely different culture, accustomed to a different kind of adversary. His ideas about warfare and the nature of conquest, and therefore his expectation of the response of others, were based in a completely different set of principles. The tragic events of the following moments in Cajamarca – and of the following months and years throughout the Andes – are thus conditioned both by the nature of the two cultures that collided and by the circumstances in which the invasion occurred.

The friar, greatly scandalized by the indignity offered to the sacred volume, stayed only to pick it up, and, hastening to Pizarro, informed him of what had been done. . . . Pizarro saw that the hour had come. He waved a white scarf in the air, the appointed signal. The fatal gun was fired from the fortress. Then springing into the square, the Spanish captain and his followers shouted the old war-cry of 'St. Jago and at them.' It was answered by the battle-cry of every Spaniard in the city, as, rushing from the avenues of the great halls in which they were concealed, they poured into the *plaza*, horse and foot, each in his own dark column, and threw themselves into the midst of the Indian crowd. The latter, taken by surprise, stunned by the report of artillery and muskets, the echoes of which reverberated like thunder from the surrounding buildings, and blinded by the smoke which rolled in sulphurous volumes along the square, were seized with a panic. They knew not whither to fly for refuge from the coming ruin. Nobles and commoners, – all were trampled down under the fierce charge of the cavalry, who dealt their blows, right and left, without sparing; while their swords, flashing through the thick gloom, carried dismay into the hearts of the wretched natives, who now, for the first time, saw the horse and his rider in all their terrors. They made no resistance, – as indeed, they had no weapons with which to make it. . . .

The struggle . . . became fiercer than ever round the royal litter. It reeled more and more, and at length, several of the nobles who supported it having been slain, it was overturned, and the Indian prince would have come with violence to the ground, had not his fall been broken by the efforts of Pizarro and some other of the cavaliers, who caught him in their arms. The imperial *borla* was instantly snatched from his temples by a soldier named Estete, and the unhappy monarch, strongly secured, was removed to a neighboring building, where he was carefully guarded.

All attempt at resistance now ceased. The fate of the Inca soon spread over town and country. . . .

During the months that immediately followed the capture of Atahualpa, Inca bearers brought an enormous ransom of gold and silver artifacts to Cajamarca. The Spaniards melted down almost all this treasure, which to judge by Spanish accounts was truly magnificent. Later other readily available gold and silver pieces that were not part of the ransom were similarly consigned to the crucible. As a result of this mania for bullion almost all the best of Inca gold- and silverwork has been lost, and there remain today only a few authentic pieces and some fragmentary though glowing descriptions of this Inca craftsmanship by the chroniclers.

plates 2, 5

Ironically, much more is known about the pre-Inca Chimú goldwork, some of which remained buried in graves and thus escaped the plundering Spaniards, than is known about the Inca gold, which soon enriched the conquering soldiers, the Roman Catholic Church and the royal coffers in Spain. The quantity and variety of the recovered earlier Chimú gold can give us a glimpse by analogy of how rich and elaborate the ceremony of the Inca court and the associated religious hierarchy must have been, especially in view of the likelihood that Chimú craftsmen would have worked for the Inca in Cuzco after the fall of the Chimú kingdom to the Inca between 1462 and 1470. Chimú goldsmiths, then, may have produced many of the artifacts later carried to Cajamarca and turned into ingots by Pizarro and his men. Other Inca artifacts, not so highly prized for the materials of which they were made, have survived somewhat better.

plates 3, 4

A little over eight months after his capture, on 26 July 1533, the Spaniards executed Atahualpa despite his having paid the agreed upon ransom. Again, Prescott gives a vivid picture of the event.[2]

The doom of the Inca was proclaimed by sound of trumpet in the great square of Caxamalca; and, two hours after sunset, the Spanish soldiery assembled by torch-light in the *plaza* to witness the execution of the sentence. . . . Atahuallpa was led out chained hand and foot – for he had been kept in irons. . . . Father Vicente de Valverde was at his side, striving to administer consolation, and, if possible, to persuade him at this last hour to abjure his superstition and embrace the religion of his Conquerors. He was willing to save the soul of his victim from the terrible expiation in the next world, to which he had so cheerfully consigned his mortal part in this.

Atahuallpa expressed a desire that his remains might be transported to Quito, the place of his birth, to be preserved with those of his maternal ancestors. . . . Then recovering his stoical bearing, which for a moment had been shaken, he submitted himself calmly to his fate, – while the Spaniards, gathering around, muttered their credos for the salvation of his soul!

The conquering Spaniards were amazed at the civilization they had discovered and were in the process of incorporating into their own overseas empire. The paved roads with elaborate suspension bridges, the vast systems of agricultural terraces, and the temples with gold-hung walls were unlike anything in Spain and bespoke a high level of technological sophistication. Yet the same people who had produced this magnificence had done so without the benefit of the wheel or writing as we know it. Moreover, in contrast to the Spaniards, they had few domesticated animals, being limited to llamas as beasts of burden, and alpacas for wool, and a few small animals such as guinea pigs and moscovie ducks, both raised for food. Yet, few though they were, these represent more domesticated animals than were found in any other part of the New World.

Because of the apparent power of Atahualpa, the Spaniards interpreted the Inca empire as a kind of uniform monolithic state with the Inca, the emperor, as its head. The interpretation with some minor variations has persisted in writings about the Inca state into the 20th century.

However, in recent years a series of Spanish Colonial administrative records have claimed the attention of some of the people doing anthropological research in the Andes. In 1962 the anthropologist and ethnohistorian John V. Murra drew attention to a very important 1562 document dealing with the area around the modern department of Huánuco.[3] He proposed that the interview and census data information contained in the document could be combined with archaeological research to throw new light on the nature of the Inca empire. In addition to the unusually good documentation, the Huánuco area also had the advantage of being an outpost of the empire which would provide the opportunity of studying the rural manifestations of the centralized administration. From this beginning a multidisciplinary project involving archaeology, ethnohistory, ethnology, and botany was started under Murra's direction, with funding from the National Science Foundation and sponsorship by the Institute of Andean Research. We undertook the archaeological part of the project, which was subsequently greatly expanded, particularly for the study of the provincial capital at Huánuco Pampa, with a series of additional grants to Morris from the National Science Foundation.

fig. 1   This book is an account of our work at Huánuco Pampa, at other sites built by the Inca state along nearby sections of the royal road, and at a series of towns and villages inhabited by the local people, mainly Chupaychu, who had

1 The Inca empire: the general area covered by Tawantinsuyu, with principal roads, sites, and the capitals of modern republics.

been incorporated into the empire. The Inca called their empire *Tawantinsuyu*, referring to the four divisions into which it was organized. It was composed of numerous ethnic groups who lived in towns and villages such as those we studied, with their highly varied styles of architecture and pottery. Our purpose was to analyze both the system of state centers that held the Inca kingdom together and at the same time to focus on the local settlements in which most of the people actually lived, maintaining a remarkable cultural diversity.

The abandoned city of Huánuco Pampa

fig. 4

Huánuco Pampa is located 150 km by road from Huánuco, the capital of the modern Peruvian department. The trip between the modern city and the ancient one traverses some of the spectacular scenery and environmental diversity for which the Andes are famous. The modern city lies in the warm, pleasant valley of the Huallaga River at an altitude of just under 2,000 m. Because of the advantages of its climate, and the convenience of plumbing and electricity, our laboratories were established there.

plate 17

plate 18

The road goes northward and westward through fields of maize and sugar cane, past the site of Kotosh, dating back to at least 2000 BC, up out of the valley floor past a village where pottery is made today. After several groves of eucalyptus trees, the environment becomes colder and more barren, the high grassland called *puna* favored by the Andean relatives of the camel – the llama, the alpaca and the vicuña. After reaching an altitude of over 4,000 m, it drops again rapidly into the valley of the Marañón River. The Huallaga and the Marañón are two of the major rivers that eventually form the Amazon. As we will see, the river systems were the homes of distinct polities in pre-Inca times, the Huallaga being occupied in part by the Chupaychu, some of whose sites we studied, and the Marañón by a group probably known as Wamali. The ridges above the Marañón Valley are dotted with many sites attesting to a much greater population in pre-Columbian times than today. During one of our trips we noted more than fifteen similar ruined villages with the aid of binoculars.

At the end of the steep ascent from the Marañón, and after a trip that varies from seven to twenty hours, depending on road conditions, the road emerges onto a remarkably flat plain 3,800 m above sea level. Looking across to the other side of the plain, a distance of nearly 10 km, a large expanse of grey stone can be seen nestled at the base of a hill. On the hill a series of dim rows look at first like outcrops of rocks. If the road and the weather have been cooperative following a morning departure from Huánuco, the final kilometers of the trip are usually traveled in late afternoon, the ideal light in which to see the dim lines on the hill transformed into rows of Inca warehouses and the masses of rock into the most completely preserved of the cities built by the Inca.

The access road for vehicles has been cut through the northeast corner of the ruins in modern times. The more proper access would have been via the main

Inca highway, entering the city from Cuzco in the southeast corner or from Quito in the northwest corner. Regardless of the entrance route, one passes between numerous buildings of fieldstone to emerge into an enormous open plaza. In the center of the plaza is a rectangular platform faced in finely cut stone. Climbing the badly deteriorated stairs on its southern side one reaches the top of the monument, now scarred by the illicit excavations of treasure hunters. From the perspective of the platform, probably used by Inca officials as a vantage point for viewing ceremonies and activities in the surrounding plaza, one can see that the city is planned in four major sections around the large central plaza. The eastern sector is the most splendid, with two huge halls, each more than 70 m long, facing the plaza. Between the slanted ends of these two structures one can see a series of trapezoidal gateways of dressed stone tracing a long passageway that connects the main plaza with two smaller plazas. While the eastern sector is the most elegant, the northern and southern sectors are the largest. The former crosses a deep gully, and the latter ascends a steep hill where the warehouses were built in neat rows to store food. In the distance to the southeast is a glistening stream fed by the spring of Wachac which provided water to the city. The western sector is the smallest, and the least elaborate but, curiously, in some respects it mirrors the eastern sector in its planning.

plates I, 23, 24

The best view of the site can be attained by walking up the hill of the storehouses. From there the whole plan of the city is spread out before one. Regularity and strict planning is evidenced in certain parts, in others hundreds of small round and square structures seem to have been placed with little forethought. In January and February, at the height of the Andean rainy season, the pampa is a lush green, but in July and August, during the dry season, and the best time to undertake archaeology, the grass turns brownish and blends with the grey stone to enhance the sadness ruins are prone to. Of course this, like any other settlement, was a mere backdrop for the people and the activities that occupied it. It is difficult to imagine it now, but in the early 16th century plazas and buildings would have been ablaze with the color imparted by the bright Inca clothing we can still see in museums.

plate II

We installed our first tent camp at the foot of the hill of the warehouses. In later seasons other camps were placed nearer the center of the site. Care was always taken, however, to locate the necessarily rather crude camp of tents and small wooden shacks so that it did not disturb a visitor's view of the ruins.

plate VIII

Living at Huánuco Pampa was not easy. Virtually all food had to be brought in. Potatoes were an exception: the soil of the site itself seems especially suited to the growing of the wonderfully flavored Andean yellow potato. The local people who made up the excavation crew also slaughtered lambs from their herds for special feast occasions. The meat, along with potatoes and spices, was baked in an earthen oven with hot stones. These feasts are called *pachamanka*, from *manka* meaning jar or pot and *pacha* meaning earth. The population on the pampa of Huánuco Pampa is very sparse and some of the excavators walked more than two hours twice daily. Most were farmers who till the soil with methods similar to those of pre-European times. Their understanding of minor variations in soil texture and color made them unusually skilled excavators. The crew also included artisans, such as weavers, who proved invaluable in recognizing artifacts as they were uncovered. There were enough musicians in the group to provide the archaeological project with its own folk band.

One of the advantages of living on an archaeological site is that one gets a feel for the climate and the overall setting. In this case, the days are warm with temperatures of more than 21 degrees Centigrade (70 degrees Fahrenheit), and the nights are cold with frequent frosts from May through September. The nearness of the heavens, with less atmosphere to filter the light of the sun and the stars, could cause a terrible sunburn by day, which was compensated by the spectacular night-time sky. Actually we seldom spent long looking at the sky at night because of the cold and the tiredness of our systems unaccustomed to the reduced oxygen. Neither the thin air nor the cold seemed to bother the local crew. They worked hard all day long and seemed amused by the gas heater that made us function in the early morning and after sunset.

The abandoned local villages of Huánuco

Our experiences in finding and excavating ancient villages of the ethnic groups which were subservient to Huánuco Pampa were highly varied and collectively somewhat different from those at the main site. The work was usually very interesting but invariably physically demanding and logistically difficult.

One of our first surveys in 1965 in the territory of the Chupaychu, one of the larger ethnic groups, incorporated by the Inca, was to the sites of Watuna and Quero. We drove to the little town of Panao, located close to Ichu, one of the very important ruins we were later to excavate, where we picked up a local plate 19 judge who was to accompany us together with three of his friends, making nine crowded into a small jeep. We drove to the end of the road, where we stopped at the house of a local farmer and had coffee. A few horses and a mule were saddled and loaded, and we started off, some of us on foot, over the high boggy plate 21 grassland, which in some ways reminds one of the higher parts of Scotland. It soon got dark and we found ourselves stumbling along in a bog and jumping streams. The mule fell and had to be reloaded in the water by flashlight. We eventually arrived at the house of a farmer where we were unexpected but the judge knew we could stay. Soon we were seated in the low, thatched, smokey plate 20 cooking hut and eating a dinner of potatoes, hominy, and coffee. In the main house nearby we spent the night in our sleeping bags on the floor on some straw while guinea pigs ran about us.

The following day dawned cold and rainy, but it later cleared and we were able to study briefly and make surface collections at both the Chupaychu sites of Watuna and Quero. These ruined villages were made up of clusters of houses built on windswept hill slopes in rolling high altitude grassland, used today and probably in the past primarily for grazing. The houses were badly fallen, but we could see that the plans were rectangular with rounded interior corners and the rooves had originally been gabled. The heavy cover of coarse grass made the collecting of surface pottery difficult, and what we found was badly eroded.

Our excavations in the village sites required greater planning since most of the ruins were located far from the roads, and all our digging equipment, food and camping gear had to be packed in by horses, mules and burros. This required arranging for an *arriero* (muleteer) and his animals in advance. We also sometimes had to secure permission to excavate on private land, and this required negotiations with the landowner, who did not necessarily live on the land in question.

One of our important early digs took place at the site of Aukimarka. We drove to the little village of Tomayquichua on the edge of the Huallaga Valley, upstream from Huánuco. There we met our *arriero* as arranged and loaded the animals with all our food and gear. The site lies on a ridge high above Tomayquichua and the valley bottom, and the ascent took us just under four hours. Part way up, one of our burros fell off the trail down a very steep, brush-covered slope and rolled a long way down. Miraculously, the animal was unhurt, but our beer supply was severely diminished.

As we arrived at the site it began to rain slightly and we had some difficulty setting up our tent in the ruins, but eventually we succeeded and were also rewarded with the view of a beautiful rainbow over the Huallaga Valley, a bright stroke of color against the earthy browns, reds and greys of the dry mountainsides. On the days that followed we could sometimes watch the airplane from Lima to Huánuco flying far below us in the Huallaga Valley. We knew that it carried the mail and news of the outside world which we would read on our return to Huánuco. Such things become important when you are in the field.

We had trouble the first day or so getting local labor to work for us in the ruins; they were suspicious and some of them fear working in the ancient villages where they believe the ancients still dwell. Soon, however, a few came and others, seeing no harm befall them, followed, and we were able to clear off the covering brush and carry out a series of test excavations. Our problem of a lack of water at the site – and that of replacing the lost beer – was solved by our laborers' bringing up these supplies when they came to work.

On another occasion when we were similarly camped in the site of Paco, this time accompanied by the late Peruvian ethnologist, Emilio Mendizábal, we had a delightful time hearing about the contemporary folklore that Emilio was gathering nearby. The fact that there were supernatural inhabitants dwelling in the site as well as ourselves was brought home to us by an old man who visited us at our tent one evening and told us that a supernatural bell lived in the site and that it rang on St John's day and, furthermore, that it would devour us if we found it. He also said that the last people who dug here, presumably either farmers or possibly pothunters, had died immediately thereafter. He added with appropriate gestures that if we slept in the ruins we would awaken without our testicles – that the spirits would snatch them away. This gave rise to some rather humorous comments on the mornings that followed. Nonetheless, these beliefs are real, the sites are the dwelling places of spirits, and the physical evidence of modern offerings to the spirits may be seen in the bottles of rum, cigarettes, and coca leaves left in the niches of ancient buildings.

In many respects the long trips away from the comforts of home and town life, sometimes coping with very difficult logistical problems of moving material and supplying a crew, tended to negate the romantic image of archaeological fieldwork. In the end what mattered most was the feeling that we were making a small contribution to understanding the achievement of a remarkable civilization. Studying the Inca gives the archaeologist a particularly good vantage point from which to appreciate the span of Andean history. This holds regardless of whether one is studying an important provincial administrative capital built by the rulers or a small village in the territory they conquered. The written record provides a context into which the sites and artifacts can be placed. It is not easy, as we shall see, but there is a better chance to reconstruct some of the details of how people lived – and occasionally to observe why they might have done what they did. Yet one realizes that the achievements of the Inca represented the culmination of more than 2,000 years of cultural development. The remains of that development are everywhere in the Andes, and the Inca can only be truly understood as part of the total story of the growth of a civilization.

In November 1532 the history of this autonomous Andean society came to an end. Although many writers and even a few colonial administrators appreciated the remarkable culture whose lands they had invaded, much in the centuries that followed was aimed at the brutal destruction and denial of its achievements. Yet Andean societies continue in many ways undaunted in the villages and hamlets where we worked. The upper level is, of course, gone. There are no Andean cities, no court life, no rich festivals for a purely native religion. But there is still a great tradition of weaving, the native languages are spoken by millions of people and there is an understanding of the environment that can only come as the accumulated knowledge of centuries.

Perhaps the greatest pleasure of practicing archaeology in Huánuco was the interest of the local people who did most of the digging. Teodocio Herrera, a weaver by trade, came and told us quietly on the second day of excavation that several of the bones we had casually put in the 'bone bag' were actually weaving tools. 'Do they need special consideration?' he asked. Later he demonstrated how the tools were used on a poncho he was weaving. It is difficult to tell which more impressed the assembled archaeologists: the smile on his face that registered his enthusiasm for working with the tools of Inca weavers or the image of the tools for an important Andean craft being used again after 500 years' rest.

One day we were digging a warehouse in pouring rain, working only because the Land Rover was coming the next day to take us down to Huánuco. We found the charred remains of stored potatoes under the charred roof of the warehouse, probably burned in the years of turmoil following the arrival of Pizarro. The potatoes were stored between layers of straw. The straw was not casually placed, but loosely woven into soft mats and bound into bales with fine rope. This technique probably encouraged air circulation, the control of which we discovered to be a key factor in Inca storage technology. But the execution was so deliberate, going beyond what appeared to have been the practical need, that it could almost be called art. Pedro Peña, one of the excavators who lived near the site, said: 'We still store potatoes this way.' He had actually stored some under a sod cover within the walls of a now roofless and otherwise abandoned Inca warehouse. We went over, removed some sod, and looked at his storage. It was similar to be certain, but much smaller and simpler in its execution. His updated observation was: 'We still store potatoes the same way, but it was very different back then.'

2 The Inca background for provincial Huánuco

The Inca kingdom flourished briefly from about AD 1200 to 1532, when it fell to the Spanish conquistador Francisco Pizarro and his 167 companions. During the last century of that span it grew into an empire covering the great distance between what is now northwest Argentina and northern Chile to the border between Ecuador and Colombia. Long and narrow, the empire embraced the Pacific coastline, the desert coastal plain, the Andes mountains and a small section of the high jungle or cloud forest of the eastern slopes of the Andes. Within its borders lay a wide variety of ecological niches related to altitude, temperature, soils and rainfall and a great diversity of people, conservatively estimated at six million. A much less conservative approximation puts the figure as high as thirty-two million.[4] Despite the diversity of people with their different languages, cultures and geographic settings, the Inca assembled the largest and most tightly organized empire in the New World. Far from being hampered by the variety, they put it to good use, devising ways to live with and exploit their varied physical and cultural environments.

Traditionally, the Inca have been viewed primarily from the point of view of their capital, Cuzco, and the ruling hierarchy. Our approach in this book, by contrast, will be to view the empire from the bottom up and from one of its outposts toward the center. We hope that this less traditional approach will cast the Inca state in a different light and perhaps reveal some hitherto neglected aspects of the way we think it functioned.

What we now know about the Inca state is derived from a variety of sources which fall into the broad fields of ethnohistory, archaeology and ethnographic analogy, each of which has its own special advantages and limitations. Ethnohistorical sources include the formal and informal accounts of the Inca written by the conquering Spaniards and their immediate descendants, and the bureaucratic administrative records resulting from the Spanish administration of the newly conquered territory and its inhabitants.[5] The former, often referred to as chronicles, were written by a wide spectrum of people, ranging from Spanish soldiers of fortune and priests to the offspring of Inca and Spaniard. They observed much of Inca life before it had been extensively altered by Spanish rule, including details of material and non-material culture which have since disappeared entirely. Yet, for reasons varying from individual to individual, they wrote selectively, often recording only what suited their own particular purposes, sometimes misunderstanding what they saw, and occasionally fabricating parts of their accounts. Nevertheless, for all their faults, the earliest chroniclers were witnesses to the living Inca culture, and many of them did their best to portray that culture accurately.

The bureaucratic records, by contrast, provide another kind of information, often more demographic or legalistic, which we will be discussing at greater length later. On the other hand, archaeology provides data on architecture, settlement distribution, subsistence, and material culture in general, a kind of information often not found in the documents or, if present, selectively treated. It is with the way documents and archaeology can be used as complementary sources that we will be primarily concerned in this book.[6]

Ethnographic analogy, the use of modern survivals of ancient customs, involves the study of contemporary anthropological research to elucidate the archaeological and ethnohistorical records. It must be used very carefully, for much has changed in the 450 years since the Spanish Conquest. Yet much also survives in only slightly modified form and can be used to broaden our understanding of Inca culture and the way Andean people have adapted to their rugged and highly varied physical setting. We speak here primarily of direct historical survivals; but careful use can often also be made of comparisons with societies in other parts of the world and the way they have responded to similar conditions and problems.

The Inca empire was a large state centered at its capital, Cuzco, in the south highlands of Peru. It had been gradually enlarged by a combination of negotiated incorporation and military conquest. When possible, Inca emissaries tried to negotiate a peaceful submission, a tactic which was often successful, especially among groups which did not have the resources to resist. Incentives to join rather than fight the expanding Inca no doubt also included the Inca policy of ruling through the existing local leadership rather than imposing their own appointees on their new subjects.

When military action was necessary the Inca relied on a large, well-disciplined army with a very well-organized supply system. Its equipment, however, was light – the principal weapons being slings, several kinds of clubs, and spears. Quilted armor, helmets, and shields constituted the main defensive equipment. Regular taxpayers made up the rank and file of the army as part of their service to the state, and the composition and size of the army probably varied a great deal according to need. *fig. 2*

The Inca took prisoners in the course of battle, but this was not the primary purpose as it was among the Aztec, who captured victims for human sacrifice. The Inca could thus devote more attention to overcoming the enemy. The discipline which characterized the army up to the point of engagement broke down in actual battle. Military actions were accompanied by a great deal of noise probably designed to bolster morale and to frighten the enemy into submission.

plate 12

Hilltop fortresses were the principal military architectural structures, among the most famous and dramatic of which was the Inca's own fortress of Sacsahuaman right above their capital, Cuzco. Sacsahuaman, one of the great wonders of Inca architecture, is built of three huge zigzag retaining walls stepped back on top of one another. Enormous boulders weighing many tons were cut and shaped to fit neighboring blocks almost perfectly. On top were towers, a water system, and other structures. The side facing Cuzco, however, was virtually unfortified because the slope was so steep it made heavy fortification unnecessary.

Of course, a large army on a campaign had to be moved, supplied and accommodated, and it was these ends, among many others, that the road system, the *tampu* or waystations, and the administrative centers such as Huánuco Pampa served. There seems to have been less physical and social separation of the military from other aspects of state life than there is in our own society, and many buildings and people could serve multiple functions. Sacsahuaman itself was clearly more than just a fortress; it undoubtedly met ceremonial as well as military needs. But, then, for the Inca, warfare itself was probably partly ceremonial in purpose. The fighting of ritual battles was a widespread Andean custom. People were frequently killed in these ritual bouts. Somewhere between games and actual battles in the later European sense, one of their purposes was apparently to help establish the political superiority of one group over another.[7]

The topic that perhaps has produced most interest in and speculation about the Inca is the political and economic organization that made possible such a large empire composed of diverse peoples and landscapes. An early-20th-century writer on the Inca, Louis Baudin, believed the Inca to be a prototype of the socialist welfare state in which the material needs of the populace were supplied out of bountiful state warehouses.[8] Others have considered the regime a dictatorship. The erroneous notion even arose that the Inca had furnished the model for Sir Thomas More's *Utopia*.

These early attempts to understand the Inca were all based on familiar European models. Modern ethnohistoric research has begun to correct some of the resulting oversimplifications and misinterpretations, but the fragmentary nature of the information about the Inca and comparable early state societies does not yet make it possible to form a very complete or precise picture of how the government and economy worked. In spite of these difficulties, comparisons with anthropologically better-known societies in areas such as Africa and Polynesia, combined with ongoing archaeological and ethnohistoric research specifically designed to elucidate economic and political matters, are substantially increasing our understanding. Most of the research reported in this volume was undertaken with questions of political and economic organization in mind.

The name *Tawantinsuyu* referred to the sum of the four parts of which the empire was composed. The capital at Cuzco was visualized as the center of the

ELQVARTOEDADDEIÍS
AVCARVNA

2 Guaman Poma drawing of Inca army (right) attacking enemies
(left) in their fortress, 'pucara'.

empire, literally its navel, with the four *suyu* or parts arranged around it. The two large sections were *Chinchaysuyu* to the north and west of Cuzco and *Qollasuyu* to the south and east. *Antisuyu*, to the northeast, and *Cuntisuyu*, to the southwest, were geographically much smaller. Some of the written sources describe an elaborate set of administrative divisions into which much of the empire was divided for bureaucratic purposes. These divisions were based on population units which were multiples of ten; the *waranqa* of 1,000 taxpayers was the most commonly referred to of such units.[9] The decimal system of administrative divisions was probably coordinated with the *khipu*, a recording device using knotted strings in a positional decimal system. In theory it provided a neat and practical basis for both Inca organization and record keeping.[10]

plate 11

There is reason to question, however, the extent to which this idealized system related to actual units in the population. The Inca used a system of colonization, an institution referred to as *mitmaq*, which enabled them to shift populations from one part of the empire to another and to break up certain groups and add to others. But in spite of the power of this device, the extent to which they had modified existing political organization and the structure of ethnically based units by the time the Spanish arrived was necessarily limited. One of the most common errors in popular interpretations of the Inca is that they are seen as ruling a monolithic and uniform state when in fact the empire was a great amalgam of units which differed in size, customs, political structure and often language.

In our opinion the formula for imperial administration and control of the provinces was not in practice absolute or uniform. It varied considerably, depending on the economic and political importance of a given region, the circumstances under which it had been incorporated into the realm and, particularly, its existing organization at the time of incorporation. The power of the Inca may in theory have been absolute, but in fact most of the day-to-day decisions were made at various local levels by local leaders who were in power at the pleasure of the Inca. In some cases the Inca were undoubtedly directly involved in selecting the local leaders, often referred to as *kuraka*. In many other cases, however, the Inca merely confirmed in power authorities who were already installed or whose selection was basically a local matter. It was in situations where the existing organization was very fragmentary or where resistance to Inca rule was strong that substantial change in local political make-up appears to have been made by the Inca.

An aspect of Inca political organization which Spanish observers recorded only indirectly, although it is very evident in the archaeological record in the Huánuco region, is the use of elaborate state-sponsored political and religious ceremonies as a way of establishing and maintaining the authority of the state over local groups. While the Spanish writers tended to emphasize military and bureaucratic aspects of control and administration, the emerging picture from the material record at Huánuco Pampa shows an 'administrative center' which was to a surprising extent committed to the ceremonial aspects of administration and to economic activities which supported them. The Inca political achievement was based on complicated administrative mechanisms which operated and expanded within a structure which was defined and regulated through ritual. Many more details of these mechanisms need to be determined before Inca political organization can be fully understood.

The economic organization of the Inca was closely linked to political structure. In contrast to Central Mexico, where huge markets offering a large variety of products were present, exchange in the Andes – at least in Inca times – was conducted mainly within the limits defined by socio-political units and in terms of rules closely related to patterns of leadership and authority. Trade in the more common sense of the term existed, especially on the coast, but its quantitative importance appears to have been minimal. Just as local political and ethnic units often retained much of their political and administrative authority under the umbrella of Inca power, they also continued to be the units within which most production and exchange was organized. Accounts which attribute responsibility to the state for feeding the population appear to be misplaced: except for certain state personnel the responsibility was shouldered at the local level.

The basic principles which governed economic matters were similar at the state and lower levels. Like other aspects of the Inca, economic organization was rapidly changing, but in 1532 it still seems to have been rooted in the deep economic traditions that also characterized the economies of small communities. One of these traditions was that of holding land in various environments. The major ecological variation in the Andes is related to altitude. Relatively minor differences in elevation translate into marked differences in temperature and rainfall producing substantial variation in plant and animal resources. The strategy for exploiting these vertically variable resources during Inca times seems to have been one of direct community control of lands in various critical habitats, rather than of loosely structured trade between the different regions. This pattern in which communities had islands providing distinct resources and thereby discon-tiguous territories is best documented for the southern highlands of Peru. It is also suggested for other regions, but it was probably less characteristic of the valleys of the coastal desert than of the highlands. This so-called 'archipelago model' of settlement and resource use gave each community access to the alpaca wool and tubers of the high altitude grassland or *altiplano*, the maize and other products of the warm valleys, and coca leaf from the moist eastern slopes. It also provided the pattern for exploiting certain more concentrated natural resources, such as salt. Such a system sometimes resulted in settlements of one or more 'foreign' socio-political groups becoming inter-digitated within lands basically controlled by another.[11]

In addition to the lands controlled by the community for the subsistence of its members, special lands were set aside for political leaders and for deities and sacred places. The products of these special lands were also in part redistributed to the populace on feast occasions, but they provided the basis for the economic support of religious and political institutions. Under the empire certain lands were assigned to the state and others to the state religion. Unfortunately we have little concrete information on either the amounts or the distribution of these several kinds of land, or the manner in which the state acquired land as it expanded. We know, however, that the productivity of state lands was often increased as the result of terracing and irrigation projects, and part of the state's strategy seems to have been to use its technological and organizational resources to bring previously marginal lands, such as those on warm but very steep valley slopes, into more effective cultivation. The state also implemented a massive storage system which enabled it to store some of its goods for long periods of time and to maintain installations and settlements in areas of low productivity.

Another basic principle of Inca economics was that taxes, and indeed most exchanges, were expressed primarily in terms of labor rather than goods. Labor was given to cultivate the state fields instead of tributes of food. In most cases the state also supplied any raw materials required and fed the laborers while work was being done. The great pool of human energy which resulted from the labor tax also provided most of the conscripts for the army and staffed the great construction and public works projects.

Most goods were produced locally, but there is evidence that the state was directly involved in the production of goods to furnish state installations and items, such as cloth, which conferred status. An important feature of both economics and politics was the giving of gifts in the name of the Inca ruler, and the state intervened in the manufacture of such goods to insure conformity to state standards and the availability of an adequate supply of items especially important in securing the collaboration and loyalty of its subjects.

Craft specialists clearly existed in the Andes from early times, as can be judged from the superb quality of textiles, metal objects and pottery. Written sources document large numbers of specialists, particularly on the coast, at the time of the Inca. However, the Inca assigned important roles in craft production to groups which were not defined specifically in terms of craft specialization. The women called *aklla*, chosen ostensibly to serve mainly religious functions, apparently spent much of their time in productive activities as will be seen below. These women performed several tasks and were not craft specialists in the usual sense; the Inca genius in manipulating various social categories toward the state's aims, however, was a basic element in their economic success.

Inca religion, like some other aspects of their culture, can be considered on two levels: the state and the local. The official state religion was in theory imposed on the newly conquered territories, but not in fact to the exclusion of the older local ones. A classic example is that of the great pre-Inca oracle shrine
plate 16   and pilgrimage center of Pachacamac, where the Inca added a temple of the sun and other appropriate imperial Inca ceremonial structures, but allowed the old cult of Pachacamac to continue. Indeed, Topa Inca, himself, the conqueror of Pachacamac, is recorded as having consulted the oracle there. Imperial Inca religion declined rapidly in importance immediately following the Spanish Conquest, partly because it was indeed imperial religion and relied on the now destroyed state structure, and partly because it was the first and obvious focus of the efforts of the Spanish priests. The local beliefs, by contrast, often survived into the 17th century, when they became the focus of a new and vigorous campaign against idolatry. Some of our best descriptions of local folk religion date from this period. Some of these beliefs and practices have even continued down to the present day in only slightly altered form.

Inca religion is not well understood, to some extent because it was so foreign

3 Guaman Poma drawing of an 'akllawasi', or house for chaste women serving the official Inca cult, with women spinning.

to the Spaniards, upon whom we must rely heavily. At the head of the Inca pantheon was apparently Viracocha, a creator, who was somewhat otiose, leaving other deities to deal with more immediate matters.[12] Of these other deities, the sun was the most important, both because of his connection with agriculture and as progenitor of the Inca royal family. Certain stars, planets and constellations were also deities, as was the moon, wife of the sun and important in Inca calendrics. The earth and the sea were also deities. In addition there were many sacred places or things called *huacas*, a term which survives today as a word for ancient mounds.

Inca ritual laid a heavy emphasis on reading omens and on divination, an interest reflected in the importance of the great oracle of Pachacamac. Much divination was not that elaborate, however, and followed methods widely known throughout the world, such as interpreting dreams and celestial events, studying the behavior of appropriate animals, and reading the pattern resulting from certain activities such as the burning of coca leaves. Some of these kinds of divination survive today; modern soothsayers read the entrails of guinea pigs or the pattern of the ashes of a burning cigarette.

Imperial ritual was very regularized. Official state religious installations had associated *akllawasi*, the houses of chaste women chosen to serve the official cult by preparing maize beer, today called *chicha*, and weaving elaborate ceremonial textiles. Identifying the actual structures associated with the official religion such as the *akllawasi* has been one of the most challenging aspects of the study of provincial Inca sites such as Huánuco Pampa.

Important Inca buildings built for state purposes can usually be recognized from their plans and often from their masonry. The most important Inca buildings were constructed of very well cut and fitted stone masonry, except in areas where other building materials were dominant. In less important parts of the sites, by contrast, the quality of construction may be quite mediocre. This generalization applies both to the heartland around the capital, Cuzco, and to provincial installations such as Huánuco Pampa. The differences are of degree rather than kind; there is much more and finer construction in the Cuzco area than at Huánuco Pampa, where the fine imperial Inca construction is limited in quantity and is good, though not outstanding, in quality. Provincial buildings were probably mostly erected by local masons working to Inca specifications with a simple technology, a situation which would in part explain the variation in quality.

plate 14

Like the architecture, Inca crafts were of a very high quality if intended for imperial use. Weaving, ceramics, woodworking, and metalwork were all carried out with great skill in the Cuzco area and sometimes elsewhere, though to the modern eye Inca artifacts may appear somewhat monotonous. Like the architecture, the crafts relied on skill of construction and plain though strong forms rather than on elaborate decoration or originality for their aesthetic impact. The contrast between the beautifully fitted yet very stark Inca architecture and that of florid, sculpturally adorned Classic Maya of Mesoamerica is striking, as is the difference between the ceramics of the Inca and those of the Classic Maya or for that matter of the earlier Andean Moche or Nazca with their elaborate and varied motifs and shapes. There is a certain Spartan and repetitive quality to official Inca state goods and buildings, but bureaucratic lack of imagination in the arts is not unique to the Inca.

plate VII

The imperial Inca ceramic shapes were copied by local potters in the provinces, perhaps, like the architecture, by Inca demand, at least for state purposes. The degree to which the local craftsmen would duplicate Inca crafts and the degree to which they retained their local traditions varied from one part of the empire to another. The specific situation in Huánuco will be discussed below, but other solutions are found elsewhere in the empire.

The subsistence base upon which Inca culture was built had been established long before the Inca and changed little under the Inca. It was in organization, elaboration and extent that the Inca improved upon the system of their ancestors. The growing of crops, principally the grains, maize and quinoa, and the roots, potatoes, oca, mashua and ullucu, was accomplished with an elaborate digging stick or foot plow (*chakitaklla*), a kind of adze-shaped hoe (*rawkana*) and a clod crusher resembling, and perhaps sometimes substituting for, a mace. Terracing and irrigation were undertaken to modify the landscape for agricultural purposes, though this appears to be more typical of the south near the capital than of the Huánuco area, where such terracing as exists is irregular, resulting more from cultivation than planning for it.

Animal husbandry, the raising of llamas as pack animals and alpacas for their wool, was practiced widely, especially in the high altitude grasslands that were not suitable for cultivation. Muscovy ducks and guinea pigs were raised for food in the home. Fishing was practiced on the coast and in some of the high altitude lakes such as Titicaca.

plate XII

This extremely brief survey of Inca culture provides the setting for our study of the Huánuco area, including both the imperial Inca installations such as the road, the *tampu* or waystations, and the administrative center of Huánuco Pampa itself and the villages of the local groups which provided the manpower for building, maintaining, and supporting the state installations.

As we noted at the beginning of the chapter, a large proportion of the common knowledge of Inca culture has been based on an analysis of the classic chronicles and on the archaeology of the Cuzco area and some provincial Inca sites. The Huánuco area offered the opportunity to study a major Inca administrative center in conjunction with the subject peoples who served it. Preservation of the archaeological sites, especially Huánuco Pampa, was excellent. Most important, however, parts of the Huánuco area had been the subject of a very detailed Colonial *visita* or inspection made in 1562 by Iñigo Ortiz de Zúñiga, and an earlier though less detailed one made in 1549. These unique documents consisted in part of a door-to-door census of certain local villages that had been under Inca rule, and in part of interviews with local chiefs who described many of the details of their religious structure, political organization, and tribute payments under Inca rule. The Huánuco area thus offered a very unusual opportunity to combine archaeological work with remarkably early and detailed documents. Moreover, the study would be able to concentrate on the relationship between the imperial order and the villages of the local ethnic groups. As side issues, we could also examine the variation between and within the ethnic groups, assess the degree to which Inca rule was visible archaeologically at the local level, and investigate the question of the degree to which known ethnic affiliation was reflected in the archaeological record.[13] In summary, our concern was with a hinterland under Inca rule, something that had not been a major concern of other research on the Inca, and we were provided with a potentially rich and virtually untapped supply of ethnohistorical and archaeological data to carry out such a study.

29

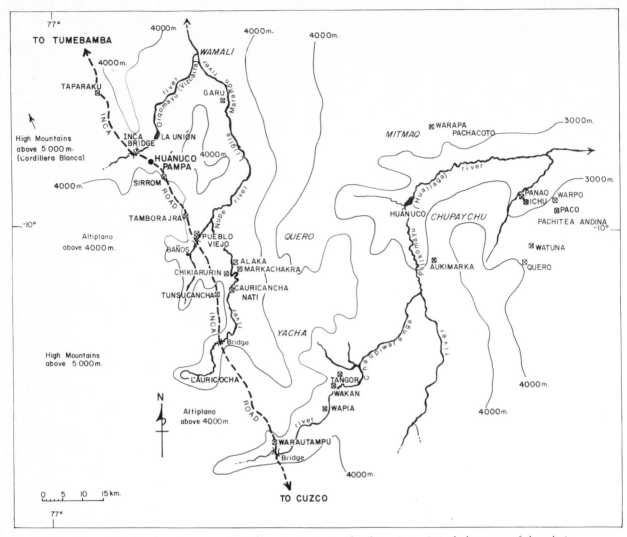

4 Map of Huánuco region covered by the 1562 Inspection by Iñigo Ortiz. It includes some of the ethnic and political groups from the days of the Inca empire. It is known from ceramics that Huánuco Pampa maintained contacts with other near-by regions as well.

3 The Huánuco region according to early historical sources

The history of the Inca occupation of Huánuco was not a blank before the initiation of archaeological research in 1964. As we mentioned, Huánuco was selected for study because of the availability of exceptionally good written sources that provided an outline of the organization of Inca rule and named key sites that could be singled out for study. A main strategy of the research was to check the accuracy of the historical data and to use them to construct hypotheses for archaeological investigation.

There are scattered references to the region in many of the standard 'chronicles' on the Inca. Since most of these sources are written from the point of view of Cuzco, they present little detailed information on provincial areas of the empire, thus contributing to an often misleading picture of uniformity within *Tawantinsuyu*. Because of the Cuzco-centric view, the information in most sources on regions far from the capital is limited for the most part to roads, administrative centers and waystations – the official infrastructural extensions of the state into hinterland regions. The pre-Inca local kingdoms that Cuzco conquered are often mentioned, but they are seldom described nor are we given details on how general principles of Inca governance may have been modified to meet local conditions.

Perhaps the best of the chronicles is that of Pedro de Cieza de León, a Spanish soldier who arrived in South America while still in his teens. After serving for a time in Colombia he moved on to Peru in 1547. The observations of the youthful Cieza are remarkable for their detachment from the European ideas and prejudices that colored the perceptions of most of his compatriots. He realized that Spanish greed for the accumulated wealth of generations in the Andes was destroying an interesting and important civilization:

traveling hither and yon and as I saw the strange and wonderful things that exist in this New World . . . there came upon me a great desire to write certain of them, those which I had seen with my own eyes and also what I heard from highly trustworthy persons . . . so, with mounting confidence, I determined to devote a part of my life to writing history, being moved to do so by the following reasons: first, because I had taken notice that wherever I went, nobody concerned himself with writing aught of what was happening, and time destroys the memory of things; . . . and second, because considering that we and the Indians all have the same origins . . . it was right that the world should know how so great a multitude of these Indians was brought into the sanctity of the Church.[14]

There is no evidence that Cieza ever actually visited the Huánuco area. The city of Huánuco Pampa would have already been falling into ruins by the time he was traveling in Peru, as was the case with the administrative center of Vilcas Waman, which he did see. Nevertheless his description, drawn from an unknown informant, of Huánuco and its principal Inca installation, is one of the best in the early records:

In what is known as Huánuco [Huánuco Pampa] there was an admirably built royal palace, made of very large stones artfully joined. This palace or lodging was the capital of the provinces bordering on the Andes, and beside it there was a temple to the sun with many vestals and priests. It was so important in the times of the Incas that there were always over thirty thousand Indians to serve it. The stewards of the Incas were in charge of collecting the regular tributes, and the region served this palace. When the Lord-Incas ordered the headman of these provinces to appear at the court of Cuzco, they did so. They tell that many of these tribes were brave and strong, and that before the Incas brought them under their rule many and cruel battles were fought between them, and that in most places the villages were scattered and so remote that there were no relations between them except when they met for their gatherings and feasts. On the hilltops they built their strong places and fortresses from which they made war on one another at the slightest pretext.[15]

Another early writer of special interest for Huánuco is the Andean native Felipe Guaman Poma de Ayala. Around 1612 he completed a 1,200-page letter to the King of Spain explaining the situation of the Andean peoples, first under native rule and then under domination by the Spanish. Guaman Poma is of special importance because he traced his Andean ancestry and heritage specifically to the general region in which Huánuco lies; his verbal and visual observations may thus reflect that area in particular. He made special reference to some Inca cities which he called 'other Cuzcos:'

there is another Cuzco in Quito, and another in tumi [Tomebamba, now Cuenca], and another in guanoco [Huánuco Pampa], and another in Hatuncolla, and another in Charcas [south-central Bolivia].[16]

His lengthy letter is important, in part, because it is from a native perspective and in Spanish heavily laced with words from his mother tongue. He illustrated his letter with hundreds of drawings, our only source on many of the visual aspects of Andean culture.

fig. 4

The major written sources on Huánuco are the two mid-16th-century *visitas* or inspections mentioned in the last chapter. Such inspections were made at the order of the Spanish Crown as part of its effort to establish control and wrest a greater share of the natives' tribute. The administrative and bureaucratic detail presented in a *visita* is in sharp contrast to the general and literary accounts of the chronicles. *Visitas* are difficult to use as sources, tedious and repetitive. However, when specific questions are being asked of them, the wealth of detail they offer more than compensates for their intractability. They include reports of actual interviews and surveys of towns. They thus have an immediacy of direct contact with the people of the time that is as close

Inca artifacts

1 A Chimú gold *tumi* or knife. This complex object from the Peruvian north coast was inlaid with turquoise stones, many of which are still present.

2 Three Inca objects of silver: an alpaca (left), a llama (center), and a female figurine (right). Llamas and alpacas are the largest domesticated native Andean animals. The llama was used as a pack animal, the alpaca for wool.

3 A close-up view of the miniature gold Inca figurine shown in color plate VII.

4 A Chimú gold funerary mask, with stone eyes and traces of red and green paint, from the Lambayeque Valley, northern Peru.

5 Two small Inca gold figurines cast in a mold. Inca goldwork is a rarity since most of it was melted down by the conquistadors.

6 Alpaca made of banded agate.

7 Typical Inca pottery, including a so-called 'aryballus'-type vessel in the center. Cf. plates 35, 36.

8 Inca stone objects, including 'star' warclub heads and stone camelids.

9 (*Left*) An Inca poncho. Such tunics are knee-length and worn without a belt. The cloth is made with red, pink, olive green, buff and gray wool wefts.

10 (*Right*) A miniature Inca poncho and bag. The checkered pattern is typical of cloth worn by Inca retainers. Bags have been used in the Andes since early prehistoric times.

11 A *khipu*, an Inca recording device using knotted strings in a positional decimal system.

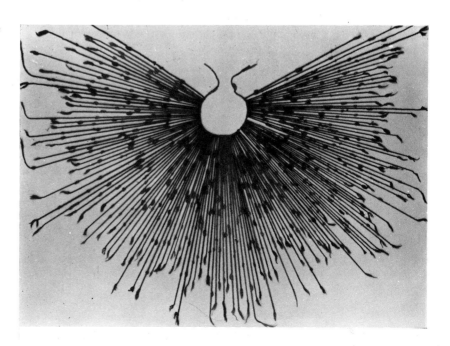

Inca architecture

12, 13 (*Right* and *below*) One of the wonders of Inca architecture, Sacsahuaman is a great assemblage of buildings within zigzag stone walls built of huge fitted and dressed boulders. It rests on a hilltop north of Cuzco.

14 (*Opposite, below*) Finely-cut and fitted Inca stonework in a wall in Cuzco.

15 Machu Picchu, one of the best
known of all Inca sites, perched high
up above the Urubamba Valley. The
semi-circular tower is built of fine Inca
masonry.

16 Pachacamac was a major Inca
center on the Pacific coast. Begun
before the Incas, it became a famous
oracle shrine and pilgrimage center.
This view is taken from the top of the
highest structure, looking towards the
sea.

The terrain

17 The warm Huallaga Valley. The Chupaychu site of Aukimarka is located on a ridgecrest like those in the background. The trees are mostly non-native eucalyptus, imported from Australia.

18 *Puna*, or high altitude grassland, south of Huánuco Pampa. Snow peaks are visible in the background, potato fields in the middle ground, and an abandoned adobe hut in the foreground.

In the field

19 A group about to leave on a visit to sites in Pachitea Andina. Author Thompson is third from the left. The judge from Panao, third from the right, is with his scribe and gun-bearer.

20 A cooking hut in which Thompson and his team ate during their survey in Chupaychu country. It was cold, foggy, and raining at the time.

21 View of high rolling country in Pachitea Andina, near the site Paco. Fields, mostly of indigenous potatoes, with some grazing sheep (a post-Conquest introduction), are visible, as are a few thatched houses of descendants of the Chupaychu.

Huánuco Pampa

22 View towards Huánuco Pampa from the south, with circular storehouses in the foreground. See also plate 53 and color plate II.

The *ushnu* platform

23, 24 (*Above*) View northwest towards the *ushnu*, showing the huge size of Huánuco Pampa's central plaza, built by the Incas to accommodate large-scale ceremonies. Cf. color plate I. (*Below*) Part of the *ushnu* platform.

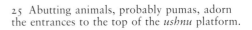

25 Abutting animals, probably pumas, adorn the entrances to the top of the *ushnu* platform.

26 A close-up view of the *ushnu* masonry, imitating the quality of the stonework of the Inca capital, Cuzco (plate 27).

27 Masonry at Cuzco: the close-fitting stonework for which the Inca are famous. At center is the famous 'twelve cornered' stone.

Gateways at Huánuco Pampa

28 View west through one of the aligned trapezoidal gateways in Huánuco Pampa's eastern section, showing the undecorated side.

29 View east through a trapezoidal gateway, looking away from the central plaza. Feline figures in relief adorn the double-jamb doorway.

30 Interior of one of the buildings of the Casa del Inca at the eastern terminus of the line of gateways. Cf. color plate III.

31 The partially dressed stones of the large halls, *kallanka*, on the eastern side of the central plaza, contrast with the Cuzco-style masonry of plates 28 and 29. Squared stones are used only at the corners. Cf. color plate V.

32 The 'incomplete temple' at Huánuco Pampa. Specially quarried stones were found between the building and the quarry. Cf. color plate XI.

33 Excavation of a house at Huánuco Pampa.

34 Wall construction of rough stones at Huánuco Pampa.

as we can come to information of ethnographic quality; the native people answer questions about their customs and activities, and a present-day investigator could potentially locate the places where they lived.

One of the inspections was made of the Chupaychu, one of the largest Huánuco groups, in 1549 by Juan de Mori and Hernando Alonso Malpartida. Although preserved only in an abbreviated form, this source is important because of its early date. Only seventeen years after the Conquest many people were still active who had been important adult participants in the local polities which were articulated with the Inca state. The brief statement about Ichu, the principal town of the Chupaychu ethnic group, is typical of the brief entries in the records available of the 1549 *visita*:

This day we visited another town that is called Ichu that is where the *cacique* [leader] Paucar Guaman has his house it has 50 houses and in them thirty four men [heads of households] and twelve widows.[17]

The other *visita*, based on an inspection by Iñigo Ortiz de Zúñiga in 1562, is preserved in a much more complete form. It is rich in detail, even though Ortiz was not well trained for his task and seems to have made his inspection rather hastily. There are suggestions that the circumstances of the *visita* may have been colored by the romantic interest of the Viceroy, Diego Garcia de Zúñiga, Count of Nieva, in the wife of the *visitador*. It has even been suggested that both the Viceroy's assignment of Iñigo Ortiz de Zúñiga, his cousin, to far off Huánuco and the latter's rather hasty completion of his job to return to Lima were related to the affair.

For the archaeologist one of the major advantages of starting out with documentation such as that found in a *visita* is that it gives us the major outlines of local level socio-political organization. This is particularly important in a complex, multi-tiered, society. The various levels and their articulations cannot be determined with any precision by archaeology alone. The information collected by Ortiz tells us which towns and villages were grouped together and something of the hierarchical organization of the various units and their leaders. Since modern place-names still reflect in various ways the names of the settlements in 1549 and 1562 it is possible to locate many of them as archaeological sites; the socio-political and ethnic structure as set down in the written record can then be compared with the material indices of it collected by survey and excavation.

As valuable as the *visitas* are, we cannot expect miracles from them. They did not ask, and therefore cannot answer, many of the questions we would pose to the people. There are two problems in particular. First, the *visitas* do not reflect a purely indigenous situation, and the influences of Spanish rule have to be constantly monitored. This is especially the case with the more thorough 1562 record, made three full decades after Atahualpa fell captive to Pizarro in Cajamarca. While complete Spanish control had not yet been effected, the turmoil of the intervening years had had its consequences, and the top levels of Inca overlordship had withered quickly.

Second, the *visitas* were made for the purposes of the Colonial regime. They were thus not very interested in aspects of native organization and administration that were not relevant to the problems of Colonial government. The questions asked in the Ortiz interviews deal extensively with tribute to the Inca. The Spanish Crown was very concerned with that topic in relation to its own levies. On the other hand, the inspection is less concerned with the nature of upper-level native administration and administrative units. An abortive Spanish settlement founded in the great central plaza of Huánuco Pampa in 1539 had been moved down from that frosty spot into the warm lower Huallaga Valley in 1541. Official interest was thus focused on the new 'capital' rather than the old. While we have some intriguing details about some of the groups that served the Inca center, our information is incomplete. We can document only part of the hinterland region that served and supplied Huánuco Pampa, and the written sources do not really define for us its sustaining hinterland.

As we shall see later, the ceramic evidence from Huánuco Pampa suggests that the Inca center maintained relationships with both the Huallaga and Marañón drainages, as well as areas to the west such as the Callejón de Huaylas. The *visitas* cover much of the most fertile and heavily populated areas of the upper Huallaga drainage. The upper Marañón region is referred to in several sources, but the information is insufficient to give a clear picture of its internal organization or the nature of its relationship to the Inca. There are references to groups such as the Yara and Huanali, but we have little archaeological or historical information on their nature or boundaries. As we shall briefly see in Chapter 8, the archaeological material associated with the upper Marañón region is spectacular, more so than that of the Huallaga basin we have surveyed. But its interpretation must await further work both in the archives and on the ground.

The part of Huánuco that is described by the Ortiz *visita* of 1562 was occupied by three main groups. The two major ones, the Chupaychu and the Yacha, were apparently native to the area, although it is probable that their social organization changed somewhat as a result of conquest first by the Incas and then by the Spanish. A third group consisted of peoples brought in from other areas and settled on lands within the territory of the Chupaychu.

The Chupaychu was by far the largest of the groups inspected by Ortiz. They mainly occupied the left bank of the Huallaga River in the modern provinces of Pachitea, Ambo and Huánuco. In 1562 the Chupaychu were organized into four *waranga*. The *waranga* was an Inca census group, theoretically composed of 1,000 taxpayers or heads of household. In 1562 Ortiz recorded 1,202 households in one *waranga*. As Murra[18] has pointed out, there is no way to determine how closely the Chupaychu may have approximated 4,000 households, nor is it likely that the forcing of pre-existing social groups into the decimal framework of the Inca census and administration could have been very precise.

The whole matter of the structure and history of formation of the Chupaychu polity is fascinating, though incomplete and unclear from the information recorded in Ortiz. A group of three *pachaca* (100 households) was apparently added to it late in Inca times. Cristobal Xulca Condor testified that 'in the time of Huayna Capac they were of the *waranga* called Yacha that was a thousand men and later Waskar Inca divided them and combined these three *pachaca* with the Chupaychus.'[19] Juan Xulca, of the town of Aukimarka, in his testimony on the size of population confirms that 'in the time of the Inca the Chupaychu . . . were four *waranga* – that each *waranga* is a thousand and the Queros that used to be called Yachas.'[20]

There is even a suggestion that the combination of the four *waranga* into a unit of related groups might have been even more recent. Francisco Nina Paucar, also of Aukimarka, testifies 'that Don Gomez principal *cacique* [leader] now deceased came to be because the *caciques* of the *waranga* died and their sons were still children . . . and after the Spanish entered this land he was made principal *cacique* of all [four *waranga*]. . . .'[21] The implication here is that the Chupaychu *waranga* were each independent until they were brought together in early Colonial times. We cannot be certain from the *visita* when the composition of the Chupaychu polity described by Ortiz for 1562 was accomplished. Did it come into being in the final years of the Inca rule, or was it an artifact of circumstances surrounding the first years of European domination? Probably there were changes during both periods, and the most important point would seem to be that the Chupaychu were a quite late political unit and that we are not necessarily dealing with a highly coherent and stable 'ethnic' group with great time depth.

The Yacha were a much smaller group. As the testimony already cited suggests, originally they had consisted of a single *waranga* which was then reduced further by the assignment of three *pachaca* of Queros to the Chupaychu, leaving seven *pachacas* of Yacha.

Economic specialists are named several times in the inspection of the Yacha. Of particular archaeological interest is the recording of potters as residents of house 32 in the town of Tangor:

In the town of Tangor the house was inspected of a man who said he was called Juan Tello Pona, subject of Don Antonio Guaynacapcha, leader of Cauri, of the same *repartimiento* of which the said Juan Chuchuyare is the principal *cacique* – he said there are in this town, subject to the said *caciques* two men, of which he in this house is one, and another named Agostin Luna Capcha, married, and another house of a woman called Angelina Chimbo, who has a daughter and a son, and the said Agostin has two daughters and a son . . .

He [Juan Tello Poma] said that in the time of the Inca his ancestors were put here as potters, being natives of the town of Caure, his and those of the said Agostin – and the woman called Angeline is from the town of Chucho – he said that these two men and the woman are counted and tribute with the town of Chacabamba which is two leagues from this town. . . .[22]

The final major group dealt with by Ortiz is the *mitmaq*, hispanicized as *mitimaes*, colonists sent considerable distances by the Inca for state purposes. The long-distance movement and settling of people in areas occupied predominantly by other groups was a common Andean custom. Its primary function, as outlined by John Murra,[23] was to give groups direct access to the resources of more than one ecological zone in the highly varied vertical Andean landscape. By establishing a series of colonies a group could assure itself a permanent and reliable access to, for example, alpaca wool from the high *puna*, maize from the deep inter-mountain valleys and coca leaf from the humid slopes of the eastern Andes. At the level of the Inca state this custom was expanded to a major mechanism of government with political and military functions. Groups that were less than fully loyal might be broken up and partially resettled among trustworthy peoples. Reliable groups were moved into newly conquered regions to monitor the progress toward Inca control.

The region around the Inca capital at Cuzco was, naturally, the most seriously affected by this practice of *mitmaq* colonization. It was the major supplier of loyal and Inca-related subjects for the outlying regions and received resettled peoples on such a scale as to change its ethnic and social landscape totally. It was from Cuzco that the major intrusions came into the Huánuco area. Ortiz inspected a group of Cuzco *mitmaq* who were settled on the left bank of the Huallaga in the vicinity of what is now the town of Acomayo. They were subdivided into two *mitmaq orejones* (big ears) and *mitmaq quichuas*; the nature and significance of the division is unclear from the *visita*. Groups were also moved in from other areas closer to the Huánuco region.

According to the testimony in Ortiz, the purpose of bringing in *mitmaq*, at least from Cuzco, was to control the Chupaychu. Don Cristobal Alcacondor of Pachacoto is recorded as saying:

[they were] put there by the Inca to guard the fortress of Catapayza that is three days by road from this town and that he [the Inca] gave them this town so they could take from here provisions and he gave and indicated lands from them, which they have now held and inherited from father to son – and that in the time of the Inca 100 married men were put in this town, and these did not tribute or serve in anything other than guarding the said fortress and making arms ohly to defend it and to hold this land because the Chupaychua were then still newly subjugated.[24]

The *visita* of Iñigo Ortiz provides an invaluable starting point for archaeology. Intriguing details are provided about many of the sites, often virtually in the words of the occupants themselves. But more than the charm of knowing the names of the inhabitants and other details, it is the information on the organization and nature of the groups that is useful to the archaeologist. For example, it would probably be impossible for us to ascertain on the basis of the material record alone that certain people had been imported from Cuzco or that the Chupaychu led by Paucar Guaman was composed of four subgroups.

It is obvious, however, that Ortiz has only provided us with a starting point. The Inca state had fallen three decades before his survey. The relations the local people had maintained with the state and its infrastructure were by then at best distant memories. The regional capital at Huánuco Pampa was a ruin and the new administrative structure was solidly centered at the new Spanish town of Huánuco in the warm Huallaga Valley. The Inca state structure is accessible only through the study of the remains of the installations it built.

Close examination of the *visita* poses questions that can only be answered through archaeology. How strongly demarcated were the boundaries of the various kinds of socio-political units outlined in the *visita*? Were the state strategic functions of the *mitmaq* colonists the only reason for their presence in Huánuco, or did they have economic functions as well? Can the probably recent date of the Chupaychu union be confirmed archaeologically? Are the Yacha and Chupaychu as different from each other as might be predicted on the basis of the great differences in their size and in the nature of the environments they inhabit? Can we find evidence of the goods they carried to Huánuco Pampa and other state installations?

5 Plan of Huánuco Pampa.

4 Huánuco Pampa: the architecture and ceramics

By far the largest and most complex site of Inca date in the Huánuco region is Huánuco Pampa. It was an important part of the network of roads and state installations to be described in Chapter 7, and was the seat from which the Inca administered the area. The ruin is located on a flat plain high above the Urqumayu River, about 12 km from the modern town of La Unión. Due to its inhospitable altitude of more than 3,800 m and its isolation from major modern roads the ancient center has remained remarkably intact. It is the best preserved of any urban-size Inca site, and certainly was one of the largest centers in *Tawantinsuyu*. Centers such as Tumebamba, Cajamarca, Sausa (Jauja), and Vilcas Waman were once probably its peers, but they all became the sites of substantial Colonial and Republican towns, reducing the Inca cities to fragments of their original plans. The ruins of Huánuco Pampa cover about *fig. 5* 2 square kilometers; the foundations of approximately 3,500 structures may still be seen, and since there are several areas where only small foundation fragments are now visible, the total number of buildings must have exceeded 4,000.

plate 33 While there are remains of pre-Inca sites on the plain or pampa near the Inca city, more than a thousand excavations in the center proper did not yield evidence of pre-Inca constructions. The Inca built their center essentially on virgin soil, and if dating of the region's incorporation into *Tawantinsuyu* is correct, construction must have begun around the middle of the second half of the 15th century. Several incomplete buildings demonstrate that construction was still going on when the functioning of the city was disrupted by the Spanish invasion in 1532. We have found no written records to enlighten us about the years just following the arrival of the Spanish, but the distribution of portable artifacts in much of the city seem to approximate their distribution during use. This preservation of Inca patterns suggests rapid abandonment rather than a shift to new kinds of artifacts and patterns of use. Several structures were burned, as evidenced by charred wood and straw roof parts lying on the floors. But there is no evidence of a general fire which could have destroyed the entire city.

We call the Inca center Huánuco Pampa to set it apart from the Spanish settlement Huánuco Viejo (or, more correctly, Huánuco el Viejo, 'Old Huánuco'), which succeeded it. The exact Inca name has not survived, but the native Andean chronicler, Felipe Guaman Poma de Ayala, includes the name Guanucopampa in his 1,200 page letter to the King of Spain.

The Spanish settlement was founded in 1539. The Very Noble and Royal City of the Knights of León of Huánuco was not to succeed, however. The exact reasons for the failure are unclear. Rebellious natives under the leadership of the famous Illa Thupa were active in the area, and there can be little doubt that the warm sunny valley of the Huallaga River was preferable for those with European habits than the frosty nights of the high altitude at Huánuco Pampa. The Spanish settlement was thus moved and continues as Huánuco, the capital of the modern department of the same name. The ruins of the original Spanish settlement, Huánuco el Viejo, are easily distinguished from the Inca city.[25] The Spanish town sits in the large open plaza of the Inca city, and seems to have been planned in terms of a grid system. It is not known why new buildings were erected in preference to re-using Inca ones. A few of the best Inca buildings in the eastern sector of the site were taken over by the Europeans, but this use may well date to a still later and very small occupation.

Pampas, as at Huánuco Pampa, are flat to gently rolling plains which occur at high altitudes in much of the Andes. They are particularly common in the region near Cuzco and Lake Titicaca, but are relatively rare at the latitude of Huánuco. It is not clear why this high location, isolated from major existing population centers, was chosen for the city. It may have been related to the pasturing of animals which were an essential element in the transportation and communication system of which the site was a part. In addition, the main Inca road from Cuzco to Quito, on which Huánuco Pampa is located, would have had to make a major detour if the city had been placed at a lower elevation. The altitude would also have been a definite advantage in the storage of food which, as we shall see in Chapter 6, was a major function of the center. However, there are many aspects of both the planning of the site and its location that do not seem to be directly attributable to utilitarian factors, and it is necessary to look beyond the materialistic explanations to which we are most accustomed in order to understand them.

The most striking feature of the material remains of Huánuco Pampa is that they are markedly different from those of the local towns and villages in the region. Both the architecture and the pottery, the only artifacts preserved in significant quantities, clearly demonstrate that the city was intrusive into a system of settlements that had been built before the Inca arrived and which continued, with only slight changes, under Inca control.

The basic quality that summarizes the physical character of Huánuco Pampa is that it imitates the architecture and ceramic styles of Cuzco. The imitations are often crudely executed, and there is certainly evidence of local influences, but the overriding impression is nevertheless one of a foreign center, built quickly according to a preconceived overall plan. The choice of building material, the size and shape of the buildings, the patterns to which buildings were sometimes grouped in walled compounds, and the overall site plan are all modifications of Cuzco construction practices, and seem to indicate a deliberate 'imperial' architecture.[26] The pottery shows the same imperial stamp. It lacks the fine execution of the Cuzco wares, but most of the forms and designs described by Rowe for Cuzco are represented in locally produced imitations.[27]

Wall construction

Virtually all the buildings at Huánuco Pampa use fieldstone quarried from a source a few kilometers east of the site. Some blocks of raw stone may still be seen on the pampa between the quarry and the city, since building was still continuing at the time of the Spanish invasion. At first glance the masonry is quite uniform. Except for a few structures of finely cut and joined stone,

plate 32

almost all of it is a double-faced construction using rough stone with a binder of earth, or earth and gravel. The exposed surface of the stones is usually fairly flat, but this seems to be the result of simply turning out the flattest surface of rather crudely broken stones, rather than of deliberate dressing. The general uniformity of the masonry is, however, broken by considerable subtle variation in detail. The size of the stones, the manner in which very small stones are used between larger ones, and the degree of flatness of the surface all vary, resulting in minor differences in the masonry surfaces. The lengthy task of studying these minor variations over a site so large has not yet been undertaken. The general impression of the site's masonry, however, is that construction was done under general, but rather loose, supervision. The basic technique is thus fairly standardized, while details of execution show both personal idiosyncrasies and the varying backgrounds of crews which were probably drawn from several different regions with varying masonry styles.

The precisely cut and fitted masonry which typifies the famous Inca buildings in Cuzco is rare at Huánuco Pampa. Where it does occur the blocks

plate 30

used are less massive and adhere to straightforward rectangular patterns rather than exactly joining curved forms, sometimes using blocks of intricate shapes. The impression is one of efficient construction of a suitable imitation, not the loving indulgence and stoneworking virtuosity seen in the capital. It is evident that dressed-stone masonry was used to define areas of the city set aside for special activities. Essentially, it was reserved for those precincts devoted to the ceremonies and rituals associated with the state, interpreted in the following chapter.

Inspection of the overall plan in figure 5, shows that the site was laid out around an enormous open plaza, 550×350 m. Dressed-stone masonry was used for the construction of the large platform which sits near the center of the plaza. The platform was probably known as *ushnu* in quechua, the Inca language. It was related to many aspects of Inca ceremonial life. The Inca, or his representative, is reported to have sat on such a platform to make astronomical observations and otherwise officiate in state ceremonies. Cristóbal de Molina, el almagrista, described *ushnu* as follows:

and in each town there was a large royal plaza, and in the middle of it was a square high platform with a very high staircase; the Inca and three of his lords ascended it to speak to the people and see the army when they made their reviews and assemblages.[28]

Large *ushnu* platforms may still be observed at Vilcas Waman, in the Peruvian south central highlands, and at Pumpu, on the shores of Lake Junin. They are all roughly pyramidal in shape and associated with open plaza areas, although none are exactly alike or even closely similar in detail. The main *ushnu* platform at Huánuco Pampa sits on two low platforms; its height above the highest platform is about 3.5 m. Steps ascend on its southern side; it is surrounded by a balustrade and may be entered through two openings. The openings or entrances to the top of the *ushnu* platform are flanked on each side by dual animal figures sculpted in high relief. The animals are probably pumas   plate 25 and are arranged so that one of each pair faces the inside of the structure, the other the outside. A similar animal, seen in profile, adorns a stone on the western side of the structure near the northwest corner.

Two small buildings on the lower platform of the *ushnu* face east and appear to relate the entire *ushnu* complex to the zone of elaborate architecture in the eastern sector. Excavations in these two structures by Daniel Shea, for the Patronato Nacional de Arqueología, encountered large quantities of decorated pottery. We did not examine the material from these excavations, but the structures may have been devoted to offerings in relation to the use of the platform.

The main platform is almost a perfect rectangle, 32 × 48 m at the base. Only the faces of the large stones of which it is built are dressed. The unexposed sides and backs are left rough and set in an earth and rock fill. The dressed faces thus create a façade of elegantly rectangular blocks. The facings of the lower platforms and the steps are not dressed. The lowest platform apparently served the function of creating a level surface on which to place the main structure. The eastern half of the plaza slopes slightly, and the lowest platform corrects this. The small upper platform was built after the main dressed stone structure. Both platforms increase the scale and impact of the structure, eliminating the impression of a simple tower-like construction in a large open space. There are some hints that a hole may have penetrated into the interior of the main structure from the top surface near its eastern wall. Unfortunately, diggings by treasure hunters have made it impossible to determine the existence of such a feature with any certainty.

Other examples of cut-and-fitted-stone masonry are limited to the central part of the city's eastern section. A series of formal gateways link that great   plates IV, 28, 29 central plaza with two smaller, subsidiary plazas and a compound of especially elaborate buildings, platforms and artificial pools. Six of the eight gateways are built of dressed stone. They are trapezoidal in shape and have a double

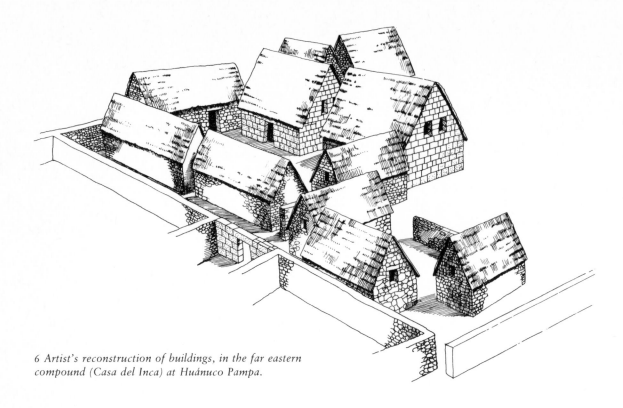

6 *Artist's reconstruction of buildings, in the far eastern compound (Casa del Inca) at Huánuco Pampa.*

jamb construction typical of classic Cuzco architecture. Each is decorated by two animal figures, nearly identical to that on the western wall of the *ushnu*, flanking the top of the gateways on the sides facing into the plazas and the compound. The gateways are so aligned that one can see through them to a point on the eastern wall of the *ushnu*. The orientation of this line is about 88 degrees east of north, almost due east-west, and is closely aligned to an equinox sunrise. It seems clear that the gateways link the central plaza with its *ushnu* platform and large halls, the two subsidiary plazas with their public buildings, and the compound of fine architecture and waterworks into a single unit. Test excavations in several places revealed a canal following essentially the same line just off the center of the gateways.

A group of six buildings within the far eastern compound is built of cut stones and is adorned with the trapezoidal niches and doorways characteristic of the architectural detail in Cuzco's best buildings. A final structure executed in cut stone is just north and east of the compound containing the bath. From the low wall height of the building, the partially hewn and cut stones lying near it, and the newly quarried stones lying on the pampa in a rough line between the quarry and the structure, it is obvious that the building was incomplete when the functioning of the city was disrupted. We thus know that this is at least very slightly later than the completed structures. In terms of care of

plate 34

plate 32
plate XI

construction and elaboration of detail, it was to have been the finest building in the city. The stones are precisely cut and joined, and its exterior was to have included several tall niches in its façade.

The elegant little building is known locally as 'the incomplete temple.' Whether in fact it was to have served as a temple is impossible to determine, but it was obviously to have become an important building, as both its location and the quality of its construction demonstrate.

The most obvious distinction in masonry and construction techniques is between the use of dressed stones with smooth faces and beveling and the only slightly modified stones set with clay referred to above. These two major types of construction are sometimes seen together as parts of a continuous wall. The gateways referred to above join onto buildings or enclosing walls of ordinary construction. The non-dressed stone masonry is rather variable. Some differences are substantial and are perhaps related to structural requirements and/or building use. For instance the two large halls on the eastern side of the main plaza are built of unusually large, rounded stones. Their walls thus have an unusual smoothness. Because of their sheer size and height, these buildings have thicker walls and deeper foundations than most of the buildings. Another apparent masonry difference is more subjective – relatively small, frequently squarish stones somewhat more regularly laid than normal, seen most commonly in the enclosure walls of large compounds such as that on the extreme northern boundary of the city proper and that at the satellite site of Wisa Jircan on the northern edge of the pampa.

plates V, 31

Building form

In his study of Inca Cuzco, John Rowe pointed out that the basic unit of Inca architecture is a rather small rectangular building.[29] These small fieldstone buildings with thatched roofs are combined frequently in groups and sometimes surrounded by an enclosing wall. They are occasionally executed in fine masonry. However, even in complex multistructure complexes, such as that of the dress-stone buildings at the eastern edge of Huánuco Pampa, the basic architectural unit keeps its identity.

Small rectangular buildings occur in a bewildering variety of sizes and orientations at Huánuco Pampa. Most of the structures in the city are built with a single door and have no preserved windows. The number of doors, however, depends on building length, and structures exceeding about 10 m generally have multiple doors. A preliminary examination of length and width measurements from various sectors of the site indicate that the range of building sizes and, especially, the average building size varied considerably from one sector to another. Data from a small sample suggest that building lengths tend to cluster around three points: 6.5 m, 7.5 m, and 11.5 m. The clusters are rather loose, and the number of buildings in the group with the greatest length is small. Width is much less variable than length. There are obvious structural constraints on building width because of the necessity of supporting the roof. The large rectangular buildings, *kallanka*, on the eastern edge of the main plaza, used columns to support their enormous roofs, showing that the Inca were capable of solving the problem. However, they generally avoided it at Huánuco Pampa by keeping building width small.

We believe that most of the building at Huánuco Pampa was done by temporary labor crews drawn from the surrounding region by the *mit'a* – the Inca form of labor tax served by heads of households for part of each year. Men from the Chupaychu, the Yacha, and other peoples in the region built Huánuco Pampa. While they were clearly following a plan and general principles approved by the state, the majority of the buildings in the city simply were not sufficiently important to receive strict supervision from state specialists. Thus there was ample room for local customs and procedures. Local influence has a variety of manifestations. The less visible apparent features of architecture and construction, such as techniques of measuring or even units of measure and shapes of stones selected, would seem to have been more susceptible to the local influences. They produce minor departures from an ideal model that could be easily ignored by a supervisor, and they involve skills learned early in life and not easily changed by casual instruction.

One imprint of local architectural custom on Huánuco Pampa may not be so subtle. Circular structures are not common in Inca buildings in most of *Tawantinsuyu*. The presence of more than 1,000 circular structures, used largely as residences, at Huánuco Pampa probably derives from the influence of local architectural tradition. As later chapters show, circular buildings were favored by some of the people who built the Inca center and later participated in its activities. Many of the circular structures are small and rather crude. They have a single door and usually lack windows or niches. Frequently a very low standing wall combined with the dearth of fallen stone about a structure suggests that the upper part of the construction was once made of a material now decomposed. Modern houses in the area often have parts of their walls made of sod; only the lower parts most liable to suffer the effects of moisture are made of stone. A similar method was likely followed by the builders of some of Huánuco Pampa's less elaborate housing.

It can be seen that construction techniques range from thin-walled structures with rather crude fieldstone masonry along the bottom and some perishable material on the upper level, through various grades of stone masonry using a mud binder, to fine-dressed stone construction, sometimes using no mud, in the Cuzco manner. The range in sizes is also great – from less than 2 m in length for rectangular edifices, to greater than 70 m. Shape, however, is limited to simple circular and rectangular forms, and buildings of multiple rooms are rare. The pattern of agglutinated architecture, with rooms of varying shapes adjoining one another and enclosing walls in a variety of ways, common in some of the local settlements of the region, is essentially absent in the state center. Architectural adornment is limited to the few examples of animal relief sculpture mentioned above. The use of niches, for both function and adornment, seems much less common than in the vicinity of Cuzco, but this is perhaps the result of generally poor preservation of upper walls.

Storehouses at Huánuco Pampa represent special variants on the standard forms of small rectangular and circular buildings. In general storehouses may be distinguished from non-storage architecture by their topographic positions and the nature of their doors. Warehousing is separated spatially on a hill to the south of the city. The buildings are arranged in neat rows following the contours of the hill, and have small window-like doors with thresholds well above the ground surface. The elaborate storage facility is discussed at length in Chapter 6.

Architectural compounds

Many of the buildings of Huánuco Pampa seem to stand essentially alone, related neither to other buildings nor to open spaces, except the areas in front of their doors, in any apparent way. Many other buildings open into plazas with which they appear to have a general association, or by the orientations of their doors seem to relate to nearby buildings. Other buildings are parts of walled compounds – well-defined architectural complexes where component structures are clearly inter-related.

The inter-relationship of architectural units is one of the most important kinds of evidence used in interpreting an archaeological site. This is especially true of a large and complex urban site. It is such relationships among buildings that allow us to identify relationships among activities and people.

In looking at the plan of the site many clear building groupings can be seen. The group of subsidiary plazas and compounds associated with the gateways in the eastern part of the city has already been described and will be elaborated in the following chapter. We select two additional, somewhat smaller, compounds for discussion here.

One of the most notable units in Inca architecture is the residential *kancha*, a group of the typical small rectangular structures referred to above. They are usually placed around a small courtyard and often surrounded by a wall. These units have received considerable attention in the archaeological literature on the Inca.[30]

Near the eastern edge of the southern sector of Huánuco Pampa is an *fig. 7* exceptionally large and complicated *kancha*. It is composed of nineteen structures and surrounded by a wall. The residential character of the compound is indicated by cooking hearths, and the pottery found in and near the structures is a typical domestic mixture of jars, plates and cooking pots. Activity differences between the various parts of the compound are still being evaluated, but present indications are that most of the structures housed generalized domestic activities with subtle differences between them.

Color plates *(pages 65–68)*

I The *ushnu*, a rectangular platform faced in finely-cut stone, in the center of Huánuco Pampa's large central plaza.

II A panoramic view over the city of Huánuco Pampa, from the hill of storehouses south of the site.

III The eastern terminus of the line of gateways leading to the central plaza at Huánuco Pampa. This compound of six small buildings of finely-cut stone may have been either a residential complex reserved for rare visits by the Inca himself or for the 'governor' who represented him. Elaborate cooking and serving facilities adjoin it.

IV One of six aligned trapezoidal gateways at Huánuco Pampa, linking the great central plaza with two smaller plazas. Built of fine Inca masonry, the gateway is adorned with two animal figures.

I

III

IV

HUANUCO PAMPA

ZONE III SUB ZONE C UNIT 4

0   5   10   20

METERS

D. Zúñiga

7 A 'kancha' in the southern sector of Huánuco Pampa. It is composed of nineteen structures surrounded by a wall.

The architecture of the compound is quite homogeneous. Most of the structures are large in comparison to others in the immediate vicinity. All except three of the eighteen rectangular houses are greater than 15 m in length and are members of the largest of the three size clusters of rectangular structures discussed earlier. Standardization of size is such in this compound as to suggest that some form of measurement was almost certainly used; it also seems likely that construction was rather closely supervised and that work was done by a single work crew.

Access to the compound and traffic flows within it cannot be reconstructed exactly. The main entrance seems to have been at the eastern end of the enclosing wall, but there may have been another access point at the western end where the enclosing wall is essentially absent. The six structures in the northeastern part are both the most regularly arranged of the complex and the most isolated from the apparent entrance. They are essentially a *kancha* within a *kancha*.

Considering the planned, state-built character of Huánuco Pampa, we might expect the classic *kancha* to dominate its architecture. In fact the *kancha* form is rare. As mentioned earlier, the great majority of common residential buildings do not seem to have been built to strict specifications, and the large number of circular houses may reflect the use of local patterns. The *kancha* discussed, and a very few others, is therefore exceptional and seems to set its occupants apart in some still unknown manner.

fig. 8

plates 42, 43

A second compound group is located at the edge of the main plaza in the northern sector. It consists of fifty buildings surrounded by a wall and represents some of the most rigorously planned architecture in the city. Relatively firm preliminary interpretations have been formulated for the function and occupation of the compound.[31] Several bone-weaving implements and dozens of ceramic spindle whorls indicate spinning and weaving as a major activity. Hundreds, if not thousands, of large ceramic jars of a kind believed to have been used for making *chicha*, the native maize beer, indicate that brewing was another major activity. Since the manufacture of cloth and beer for the state is attributed in the written sources to women known as *aklla*, it is at least a reasonable hypothesis that a group of these women occupied the compound. The *aklla*, frequently referred to as 'chosen women' in the popular literature, were selected for state service usually when young. They were reputedly of great beauty, spent some of their time in religious service and maintained their virginity – at least until the Inca honored a loyal follower by offering an *aklla* in marriage. Several characteristics of the architectural and archaeological records corroborate the *aklla* hypothesis. First, access to the compound is tightly controlled. The only entrance is a narrow door in the southern side of the enclosing wall. After entering the compound one passes through a small courtyard onto which opens a single building, unusual because its door is in its end. It is then necessary to go through a tiny square building to reach an open courtyard, that appears to have been the essentially public area of the compound. The apparent emphasis on control and security is in keeping with our expectations of seclusion for the 'chosen women.' The regular rows of rectangular structures in the northern part of the compound constitute a kind of barracks-like architecture, suggesting a non-family occupying unit. The great density of refuse in the compound suggests permanent occupation and contrasts with the small amounts of refuse in much of the city implying temporary occupation.

If we eliminate the structures immediately associated with the entry area, the long buildings opening onto the interior courtyard, and the small buildings in the middle of some of the streets of the compound, the remainder of the buildings are very standardized in size and form. A group of thirty-one structures ranges in length from 17.8 to 19.1 m, with an average of 18.2 m. A second group of seven buildings on the western side of the compound is somewhat shorter, but also with nearly identical lengths, averaging 13.7 m. All the buildings of both groups had two doors, with one possible exception.

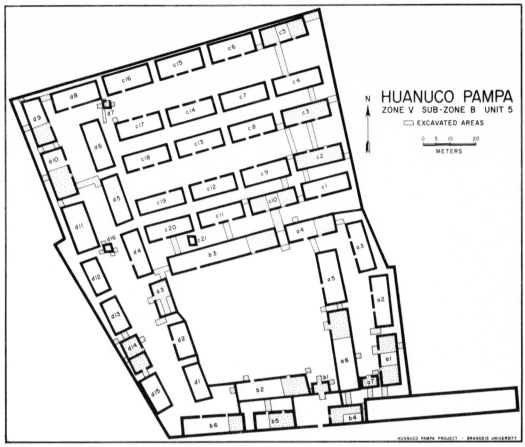

8 *A compound of fifty buildings at the edge of the main plaza in the northern sector of Huánuco Pampa. It represents some of the most rigorously planned architecture in the city.*

Artifacts hint that there may have been minor variations in the activities associated with the buildings; all apparently served as both residences and workshops. The difference in size between the two groups probably reflects the necessity of accommodating the buildings to the trapezoidal space of the compound, not to the difference in function.

Present interpretations of traffic flow and activities within the compound suggest that the buildings near the entrance related to monitoring access and perhaps to administering the activities within it. The open courtyard and the larger buildings surrounding it suggest a more public space than the rows of residence-workshops that comprise the greater part of the compound. These suggested differences in activities require further verification by ongoing studies of artifact distribution, but we can begin to see an emerging picture of how common architectural units could be combined in quite complex ways and, at the same time, how common daily activities could be combined and put in a new context for the state and its city.

The city plan

We have no doubt that Huánuco Pampa was constructed according to an elaborate preconceived plan. As noted, the nature and placement of many individual buildings is irregular and not carefully planned. But, as a whole, the site follows a pattern of organization that gives it a series of recognizable divisions and results in what, to modern eyes, is an unusual shape.

We have already described the enormous open plaza and the *ushnu* platform which are the city's center. Radiating out from that center are a series of streets, open spaces and walls. These essentially form 'lines,' some clearer than others, that divide the site into several discrete zones. One of the most obvious of these divisions is the main Inca road, the *qhapaq ñan* – which passes through Huánuco Pampa on its Cuzco to Quito route. The road, crossing the city diagonally in a southeast to northwest direction, in effect cuts the city in half. Other lines extending from near the northeast and southwest corners of the plaza combine with the *qhapaq ñan* to divide the city plan into four parts. As figure 5 shows, other walls and streets further divide each of the four divisions into three parts, creating a total of twelve sectors.

A few of the dividing lines are somewhat indefinite, and there are some grounds for challenging the divisions as representing a clear Inca plan. The divisions were originally made for purposes of designing the sample for excavation and for the enormous task of establishing a recordkeeping system for a large, complicated site with over 3,500 structures. A site so large must be broken down so that one area may be compared with another in a general framework for excavations and other studies. By carefully looking at the architectural layout, an attempt was made to divide the site into a set of areas that conformed as closely as possible to the Inca pattern of design and use. We sought to arrive at divisions that were culturally meaningful, analogous in a sense to the stratigraphic divisions into which deep sites are divided vertically. However, the meaning of the cultural divisions are obviously somewhat different in this case.

A few years after the initial preliminary map was completed and the site divided into architectural zones, a close parallel was noted between the spatial pattern emerging from the city plan and the pattern of arrangement of the shrines or sacred places, called *huacas*, in the vicinity of Cuzco. The shrines, which included a variety of natural and man-made sites, were listed by Bernabe Cobo[32] in the 17th century and analyzed by Tom Zuidema.[33] A series of structural, organizational principles emerge from the system of *huacas* which seem to permeate several aspects of religion, social organization and relate to the Inca calendar. The emphasis on dualism, tripartition and quadripartition results, in simplified form, in the division into an upper (*hanan*) and a lower (*urin*) part; the parts are each then further subdivided into two parts each. The four resulting parts are each divided into three. Such a system results in a total of twelve units. The *huacas*, or shrines, form twelve main groups; there are certain complications regarding uneven numbers of shrines in some groups. There are also multiple perspectives from which the Inca apparently viewed their organizational principles, and at least two of these may be apparent in the urban plan. These problems need not detain us here. (If the interested reader wishes to pursue the subject, Morris[34] has written on it in more detail.)

We do not imply that the twelve divisions of the plan of Huánuco Pampa are necessarily related to shrines, only that the city was laid out in accordance with principles of structure and organization that are analogous to those that govern the system of lines (called *zeques*) that organized the shrines. We suspect that what is being structured here is not shrines but social groups. In other words the city plan somehow reflected symbolically the positions and inter-relationships between the groups which occupied it. These inter-relationships are the subject of studies still in progress using the Huánuco Pampa data files. Such studies are quite difficult since we have no good measures by which to identify the component groups. According to the written sources, clothing was the obligatory indication of group differences. It included required insignia by which a person's affiliation was readily identifiable. The humid soils of Huánuco Pampa do not preserve this prime carrier of the labels we need. Broken pottery vessels are what we have in abundance, but as we shall see presently they are an imperfect and difficult to use index of social and ethnic group composition in an urban context.

Pottery

Few, if any, sites in the Andes have provided their excavators with as many sherds of pottery as Huánuco Pampa. Our excavated sample in and around approximately 300 structures produced more than 15 metric tons of pottery. The deluge of material caused constant logistical problems during excavation. On more than one occasion a truck had to be contracted to transport the backlog of accumulated sherds from the storage tents at the site to the laboratory. Because of a lack of adequate facilities near the ruins, the laboratory was established in the city of Huánuco, 150 km away. The ceramic analysis is still underway. The archaeological adage that at least two months analysis time be allotted for each month of excavation proved to be an underestimate of the wealth of material at Huánuco Pampa.

The study of the great masses of pottery left by the occupants of the Inca center had two primary aims. First, we hoped to use ceramics as an indicator of the presence in the city of various ethnic groups from its hinterland. Second, we studied the sherds from the point of view of function; how could the kinds, sizes and quantities of pottery in various parts of the city give us information on the activities that took place?

At the very outset of research the primary characteristic of the ceramics became clear: the vast majority of the vessels were made to imitate the shapes and forms of Cuzco pottery. This was in dramatic contrast to the pottery from the towns and villages known from Iñigo Ortiz to have served Huánuco Pampa. As we shall see in Chapters 7 and 8, local pottery imitated Cuzco ceramics in only very minor ways, being characterized mainly by a continuity from pre-Inca traditions. Just as most of the architecture differed, except in subtle ways, from the architecture of the countryside, the pottery was produced in terms of different criteria. Only the pastes and other material and technical aspects were shared in the vast majority of the cases. The differences are so marked that we feel Huánuco Pampa, Tunsucancha (which has stylistically nearly identical ceramics) and some of the other installations were provided by the state with pottery that symbolized Inca power and control.

While the overwhelming emphasis on Cuzco imitations is interesting in itself, it means that the ceramic collections from Huánuco Pampa are very difficult to use to measure any kind of 'ethnic' presence in the city. However, as work progressed, it became apparent that ceramics of the local peoples were represented in very small proportions, often less than one percent, never more than five percent in any given building. It was only as our ability to distinguish some local plain wares from undecorated Huánuco Pampa material increased, and the number of sherds studied passed into stratospheric levels, that we could have some hope of evaluating the presence of local peoples in the state's city. The relatively higher proportion of local wares in certain areas of the city probably suggests more frequent contact with the towns and villages known to have 'served' Huánuco Pampa. The especially low occurrence of local wares in the buildings near the complex of gateways and in the compound thought to have been occupied by the *aklla* is important. It probably reflects permanent residence by people directly engaged in state-related activities. Because of the extremely large samples involved these differences seem significant, even though the differences in the percentages of local sherds is only in the magnitude of one or two percent. Another way of looking at the matter is to note that the percentage of local sherds in certain areas of the city is more than twice that in other areas, even though the absolute percentages are always small.

The second aim of the pottery studies, to identify activities and patterns of residence, looks at somewhat different characteristics of the vessels than those used in attempting to identify socio-political groups. While stylistic features and details of manufacture have been most useful in separating the pottery of one group from that of another, we expect shape and size to be the best indicator of vessel use. Most ceramic vessels, of course, have relatively generalized functions as containers. They hold different things at different times, and combine with other vessels and artifacts in a variety of complex activities. It is mainly these complex activities, such as cooking, brewing and long-term storage, that we wish to identify.

In principle, the functional study of ceramics is very simple.[35] We examine the distribution of the various shapes and sizes of vessels over the city. It is a

9 Decorated Inca pottery fragments found at Huánuco Pampa.

10 *Cuzco-Inca pottery shapes also found at Huánuco Pampa.*

matter of seeing how many cooking pots, large jars and plates are found in one area in comparison with other areas. In practice, this study is very time consuming given the size and enormity of the sample. A computer must be used to process the collection. Several years have been spent recording and entering millions of points of data on computer files. This analysis is still underway.

Fortunately the shapes of Inca ceramics are remarkably standardized. In most cases the form of the entire vessel can be determined from a large rim sherd. The shapes found in Huánuco Pampa are variants of the shapes found in Cuzco. In comparison with many other provincial regions of *Tawantinsuyu* the replication of Cuzco forms is quite exact. It is still easy to distinguish between the two, however, particularly when whole or nearly whole vessels can be restored. The proportions of the bodies of the vessels are noticeably different. The form of large jars generally called 'aryballoi,' for example, tend to have more globular bodies and rounded shoulders in Huánuco than they do in Cuzco. The use of the term 'aryballoid' for these vessels is inappropriate, since they differ substantially from the Greek vessels of that name. We have used a more neutral system of numbers; large jars with a narrow neck and a pointed base are called simply Form 1.

Huánuco Pampa lacks a few of the shapes found at sites in the vicinity of Cuzco and has a few additional ones. Nevertheless, the range of shapes is similar. Besides Form 1 jars there are other jars with wider mouths (Form 3), the well-known pedestal base pot (Form 7), a huge pot-like vessel with a pointed base (Form 8) and several plate forms (Forms 13, 17, 18 and 19). The

fig. 10
fig. 9

plate 36
plate 38
plate 37

plate 39

	Narrow-mouth jars (Form 1)	Wide-mouth jars (Form 3)	Small pots (Forms 6 & 7)	Large pots (Form 8)	Plates (Forms 13, 17, 18 & 19)
East-Central (IIB)	32.6	11.2	8.5	7.0	23.1
West-South (IV,A)	47.5	4.9	12.7	3.5	17.7
North-Central Unit 5 (V,B5)	42.6	10.6	11.4	2.7	22.2
Far North-West (VI,A)	38.6	3.7	9.1	1.7	42.9
Far South (VIII,B)	93.7	.0	4.8	.0	1.5

Table 1

division into major functional classes of jar, pots and plates is based on simple principles of constriction and the ratio of height to diameter. Jars are much taller than they are wide and relatively constricted. Pots, exclusive of pedestals, are wider than they are tall and only slightly constricted. Plates are much wider than they are tall and unconstricted, that is to say their maximum diameter is at the mouth. Table 1 shows an example from preliminary and partial data of how some of the major functional categories vary in different parts of the site. We have divided jars into the categories wide-mouth (Form 3) and narrow-mouth (Form 1). We believe this distinction is significant in terms of use, with the narrow-mouth jar being used mainly for serving and storage and the wide-mouth used frequently for brewing and perhaps other forms of large-scale food preparation.

Table 1 is based on the study of just over 20,000 rims from several parts of the site. The sample from each area mentioned is at least 500 vessels, but we caution that some of the areas have much greater architectural variety than others, and the various ways ceramics relate to this architectural complexity cannot be taken into account here. The table demonstrates that the shapes of the vessels do indeed vary from one zone to another. In some cases characteristics of architecture or other finds associated with the ceramic configurations help us understand them and suggest the activities in which they were used.

The most obvious occurrence in the table is the 93.7 percent of wide-mouth, Form 1, jars for the far south sector. That is the storage zone, and is discussed in detail in Chapter 6. Another area of the site for which the proportions of

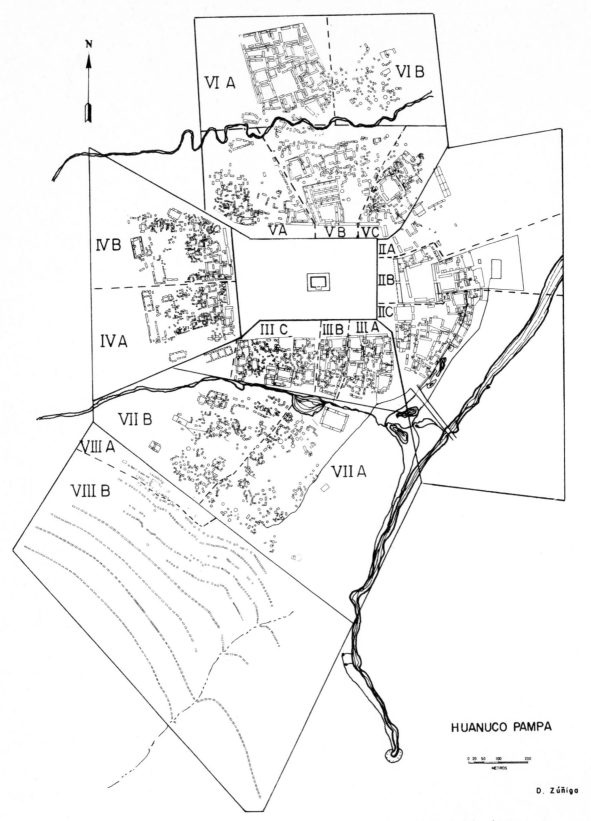

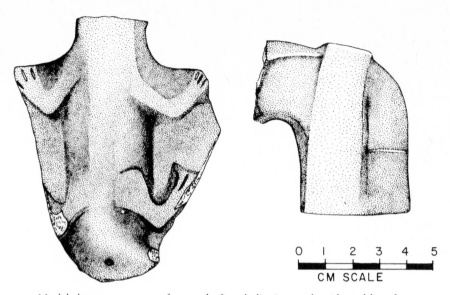

12 Modeled pottery creature frequently found clinging to the side and lip of a drinking vessel ('kero'). At the left is a view of the body, at the right a side view of the head as it would have extended above the vessel lip. The modeling probably represented a feline.

vessel shapes are notable is less easy to explain. The western part of the far northern sector (Zone VI, A), a walled compound of large rectangular structures, is characterized by a very high percentage of plates and an unusually low percentage of pots and wide-mouth jars (Forms 3, 6, 7 and 8). If our assumptions regarding vessel function are accurate this would tend to suggest an emphasis on serving food and drink but not on cooking or brewing. When taken together with the architectural suggestions of large buildings in a well-planned unit and the lack of sherds, the compound gives the impression of having been a barracks-like facility in which people ate and presumably lived, but did no substantial amount of cooking. As very few spindle whorls and no shawl pins were found, the occupants or users may have been predominantly or entirely male. No evidence for specific economic activities was revealed in the excavations in the compound, and at this point it is difficult to match the use with any specific group of residents outlined in the written sources.

The architecture of the central part of the eastern sector (Sub-Zone II, B), and of the compound (Unit V, B5) north of the plaza where we believe *aklla* weavers and brewers lived, has been described above. Table 1 demonstrates that both of these areas have a larger than usual percentage of wide-mouth (Form 3) jars. Our interpretation of both these areas as being involved with brewing and large-scale food preparation has already been pointed out. The proportions of vessel forms, however, suggest some differences between the two areas. Most significant are the contrasts in pot forms. The buildings around the plazas of the eastern sector produced a higher than usual

fig. 11

plate 4

fig. 12

79

percentage of the Form 8 vessels, which tend to be very large. In the compound with the weaving evidence, most of the pots are much smaller, Forms 6 and 7. This evidence seems to imply that while brewing was carried out in both areas, certain significantly culinary activities in the compound of the weavers was carried out on a much smaller scale. The most likely interpretation of these vessel configurations would seem to be that cooking for smaller units, i.e. the residents of the compound, was part of the activities of the weavers. The more public buildings in the eastern sector, on the other hand, perhaps saw exclusively large-scale preparation and serving of food and drink. One was primarily a public area; the other involved brewing for a larger number of people than lived in the compound, but it also involved smaller-scale cooking for permanent residents.

Data from the western part of the site and parts of the zone just south of the central plaza look rather more like what we would expect for the food preparing and consuming pattern of household-sized units. Table 1 shows the percentages for the southern half of the western sector (Sub-Zone IV, A). The percentage of narrow-mouth, Form 1, vessels is not greatly different from several other areas. Small pots (Forms 6 and 7), however, represent a greater part of the vessel assemblage, and the wide-mouth jars (Form 3) that we associate with *chicha* making are less common.

The basis for understanding the role of Huánuco Pampa in the Inca scheme of rule and in the economy and overall organization of the Huánuco region is the reconstruction of activities. Buildings, groups of buildings and whole zones must be looked at in detail. The association of certain characteristics of pottery with certain types of buildings and open spaces and with other finds are the archaeological raw materials from which such reconstructions are made. But, as we have seen, the interpretative process involves a constant interplay between a series of models for various aspects of Andean society and economy during Inca times. It is constant balancing of similarities and differences, always difficult and sometimes only partially successful. However, these are the only means available for studying societies that left little written information. We have been able to present only a small part of the actual archaeological detail here, but it should serve as a basis for a preliminary evaluation of the city, to which we now turn.

5 Economy, ritual, and the politics of provincial administration

It has long been apparent that Huánuco Pampa and other large centers on the Inca road system were somehow related to the integration and administration of the empire. However, these cities were either abandoned or converted to Spanish purposes and control soon after 1532. The written evidence on their residents and the way they function is, therefore, extremely fragmentary. Lacking specific information on these centers we have tended to interpret them in terms of ideas derived from our knowledge of the functioning of modern states. We have often imagined them as state settlements filled with bureaucrats, provincial governors and the army. They were places where local decisions were made, and the will of the rulers in Cuzco was carried out. A strong military presence was thought to have been an essential element in backing up the state's policies and insuring fulfillment of the economic obligations that allowed the state to operate.

Beginning with a survey by both of us in 1963 and 1964 and followed by the intensive mapping and excavation projects directed by Morris in the 1970s, much of the archaeological data we collected was sought specifically to help answer the question: 'What was the Inca administrative center like and how did it serve as a link between the state and ruled peoples?' Although final analysis of the results is incomplete, the outlines of an answer to that question are beginning to emerge. They leave little doubt that our basic assumption about the primary function of Huánuco Pampa as a center of administration is correct. We have revised substantially, however, many of the specifics regarding the nature of that administration and the context in which it occurred.

Anthropologists have been aware for many years (Mauss; Polanyi; Barth) that in most societies many aspects of what we consider economics, politics, religion and even kinship are inter-related or imbedded in each other. It is therefore difficult to analyze the various institutional aspects separately. It has been implicit, however, in the thinking of most social scientists that, with increasing complexity, societies develop specialized institutions which separate out various kinds of functions. With the increase in specialization of institutions comes an increasing specialization of the roles or jobs and activities of the people, and also a tendency for some people to be wealthier and wield more authority than others. This division of a populace into specialized roles, statuses and ranks is a hallmark of complex societies.

Given the fame of the Inca for their control of a vast territory, the development of a complex system of roads and communication and the mastery of a series of technologies that, for their day, were very advanced, we have become accustomed to think of the Inca as a powerful state society well along the scale in terms of increasing specialization of institutional functions. After all, no truly primitive society could build and maintain 14,000 miles of roads or fill what must have been at least 10,000 warehouses.

John Murra's classic analysis of the Inca economy[36] based on the sources available to him revealed that economics and politics were still closely bound together and that, in apparent contrast to the other major New World center of civilization in Mexico, markets and trade in the normal sense played a minor role. His work demonstrated that when one looks at the difficult written material on the Andes as an ethnographer, as unbiased as possible by our own ideas of western society, one sees a rich and elaborate set of institutions that show some similarities to historically known states in Africa and elsewhere, but are also in most ways peculiarly Andean. As we begin to see a more direct picture from the archaeology of Huánuco Pampa, we believe that there is indeed a high degree of institutional specialization among the Inca, but that the specific character of the institutions remained Andean and was grounded in long tradition. It is also evident that Inca institutions were undergoing rapid transformation. It is difficult to chart the nature and direction of that transformation with the data in hand. However, we do not see in the evidence from Huánuco a trend that would soon lead to a clear separation of economic and political institutions or to the creation of an administrative center which was based on impersonal and bureaucratic sorts of procedures.

Before reviewing more of our current reconstructions of the activities in Huánuco Pampa and our interpretations of their meaning in terms of the administration of the Huánuco region in particular and *Tawantinsuyu* in general, it is necessary to stress two important caveats. First, we remind the reader that only about eight percent of Huánuco Pampa's buildings and less than two percent of its surface area have been tested and that analysis of even that material is still underway. Second, while we have visited the ruins of several other administrative centers which may have played a similar role in co-ordinating the Inca empire, none has been studied in detail. It would, therefore, be ill advised to assume that Huánuco Pampa is typical of a large number of 'administrative capitals' throughout various parts of *Tawantinsuyu*. While we suspect the activities we see here must also have taken place in many other locations, their exact nature and the ways they were combined were probably influenced by numerous local factors. The limited evidence from the sites we have visited certainly suggest great regional diversity. John Hyslop has shared with us some of the information from his recent survey of the Inca road systems that took him to many different areas of the Inca territory. He stresses diversity as one of the main characteristics both of the roads and the sites that lie along them.

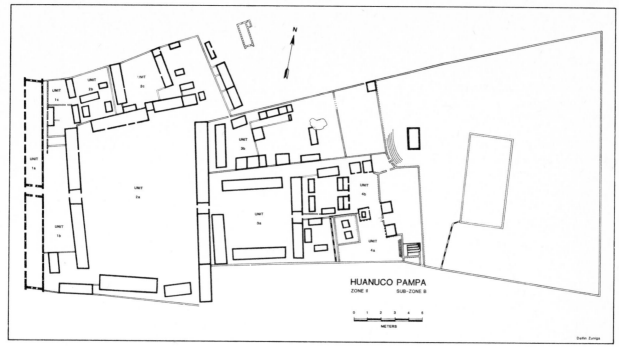

13 Zone II, B on the eastern side of Huánuco Pampa. Evidence of feasting, and related ceremonial activities, comes from this set of architectural compounds and spaces connected by gateways.

Ceremonial activities and political functions

It was common in the archaeological literature of a couple of decades ago to refer to 'ceremonial centers.' The definition of such centers was, perhaps deliberately, usually left vague, but the general idea was that they were centers to which people came seasonally to participate in ceremonies of a primarily religious nature. They were thought to lack solid institutions of political leadership. These 'ceremonial centers' were contrasted with urban centers where populations were both permanent and relatively large, and the activities usually included markets, manufacturing, and basically secular mechanisms of rulership.

We do not want to imply that Huánuco Pampa was only a ceremonial center in that somewhat dated use of the term. Nevertheless, the archaeological evidence does point to a clear emphasis on activities of a ritual or ceremonial nature. Furthermore, we suspect that most of the participants in these ceremonies and rituals were not permanent residents of the city. The point is that the rituals involved were a key aspect of administration.[37]

The evidence for the predominance of feasting and related ceremonial activities comes mainly from the set of four architectural compounds or spaces

Color plates *(pages 85–88)*

V   A *kallanka*, one of two large halls on the eastern side of the main plaza at Huánuco Pampa, is built of unusually large, rounded stones.

VI   Inca poncho of the Colonial period from Murokato, an island in Lake Titicaca, Bolivia. In the lower part of the garment the threads are interwoven with gold.

VII   A miniature gold Inca figurine with poncho, bag, and wrapping. This assemblage was probably made for some ritual use. Similar items have been found buried above 5,500 m on Andean mountaintops which served as sanctuaries.

VIII   Fieldcrew at Huánuco Pampa. Approximately 1,000 excavations were made at the site, testing about 8 percent of the buildings.

IX   Circular houses at the Wamali site of Garu. The walls are up to their original height and they recall the pairs of circular houses at the site of Aukimarka.

X   Storehouses (*qollqa*), undoubtedly of Inca date, below the Wamali site of Garu. They recall the local village *qollqa* at Aukimarka.

XI   This building of fine Inca stonework within the far eastern compound at Huánuco Pampa was to have been one of the most important constructions at the site. It was not complete when the city's activities were disrupted, and its exact function is unknown.

XII   Andean camelids (llamas) in a high plateau region.

XIII   Rows of Inca storehouses (*qollqa*) are just visible on the hillslope south of Huánuco Pampa. Their capacity is over 35,000 cubic meters.

XIV   Inca silver llama found near Lake Titicaca, Bolivia. The red blanket is inlaid with gold and cinnabar.

V

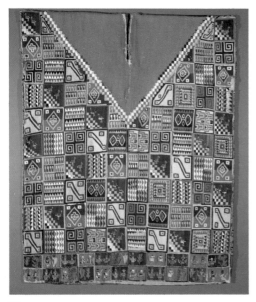

VI

VII

VIII

IX

X
▼

XI

XII

XIII

connected, and presumably inter-related, by gateways as described in the preceding chapter. They consist of the main plaza in the center of the site, the two subsidiary plazas to the east and the compound of elaborate architecture and waterworks terminating in a 'bath' on the eastern periphery. The evidence consists of the architectural character of these units and the ceramics and other materials associated with them.

fig. 13
plate 47

The architecture is clearly on a monumental scale and is arranged to provide large spaces, both interior and exterior, that are capable of accommodating substantial numbers of people. The use of fine Cuzco-style dressed masonry on the face of the *ushnu* platform, the interior gateways and some of the buildings in the far eastern compound set the area apart in terms of the special nature of its construction and its imitation of, and symbolic link with, the capital of Cuzco. The sector is therefore both public and clearly state-related in nature. It is a prime example of what Gasparini and Margolies[38] have characterized as the 'architecture of power.'

A scheme was set up for sampling the open space of both the large main plaza and the two secondary plazas. The early results from the tests were so uniformly disappointing, however, that the sampling plan was discontinued. Cultivation at various points during the history of the site after its abandonment appears essentially to have eliminated any significant evidence of activities in the large open areas. We did determine that the main plaza, especially on the east side, had been partially leveled by filling with a mixture of earth and small rocks.

Excavations in one of the two enormous halls or *kallanka* at the east of the main plaza were also disappointing. The entire 65×12 m structure was cleared. Down the center of the structure we uncovered a row of large postmolds surrounded by stones, confirming that the roof was supported by interior columns. Only a few dozen small pottery fragments were found. They were too few and too small to be any indication of the use of the structure. Vásquez de Espinoza passing through Huánuco Pampa in 1616 observed that the two buildings were being used as stables. That use had apparently obliterated all significant remains of Inca function in the buildings studies.

There were many buildings all around, beginning with two *galpones* or halls so large that each was the size of a race track for horses, and with many doors; this must have been where the leading Indians, and the lords representing the kings, were lodged, at present they serve as cattle corrals.[39]

The excavations in several other structures surrounding the main plaza and the two subsidiary plazas were much more rewarding. Undoubtedly the artifacts were re-arranged somewhat during Spanish times from their Inca patterns of distribution. However, with a couple of exceptions, the European disruption appears minor and does not seem to have produced large-scale disturbance of artifacts, and the excavation results are probably quite accurate reflections of the ceramic vessels used in and near the buildings.

The principal result of the tests was that great masses of pottery were found, especially in the buildings around the secondary plazas. There was also a substantial amount of faunal and botanical material, still being analyzed. But, as the chart in the preceding chapter shows, in general the material is characterized by a predominance of jars, including much higher numbers of wide-mouth jars than usual. The proportion of plates is also slightly higher than in most areas of the city. Overall vessel size is considerably larger than average.

Pat H. Stein, who supervised the excavations and study of the material for the Huánuco Pampa Archaeological Project, interprets this combination of materials as evidence for large-scale food preparation and, especially, serving. The large vessel size suggests that the facility was used by substantial numbers of people at the same time. The complex of jar types and sizes is reminiscent of the vessels still used in the production of *chicha*, the New World maize beer. The circumstances of burning associated with one of the structures in the interior plazas produced a large fragment from an Inca *kero*, a wooden drinking vessel. A cache found in a stone niche beneath one of the thresholds of the same building contained several intact ceramic vessels along with wooden plates – preserved by the dry conditions in the protective niche. These special accidents of preservation demonstrate that many of the objects connected with consumption of food and drink are perishable and are not normally found. They also complement the ceramic assemblage from the area, adding to the evidence for the provision of food to multitudes of people.

plate 50

plates 40, 49

The differences between the buildings adjoining the three plaza areas require much more detailed evaluation. However, the material near the main plaza is much less concentrated than that associated with the interior ones. The tendency for the largest amounts of material to be concentrated near the doors of structures suggests that much of it may have been connected with activities which took place outside in the plazas. Of course, this might also be somehow connected with the pattern of abandonment rather than use of the site, but the occurrence is such a regular one that it seems unlikely to have resulted from the less controlled behavior we expect from situations of abandonment.

A Spanish occupation and recent treasure hunting have seriously distorted the archaeological evidence in the compound at the eastern terminus of the line of gateways. One of the buildings seems to have served as a smithy in Colonial times, but artifacts associated with the area in general do not provide a reliable indication of Inca use. On the basis of architecture, we believe the group, essentially a *kancha* of six small buildings of finely cut stone, may have been either a residential complex reserved for rare visits by the Inca himself or for the 'governor' who represented him.

plate III

The fact that the elaborate cooking and serving facilities adjoined the compound that possibly served as royal quarters indicate that they were a vital element in the whole system of Inca provincial administration. The relationship between the rulers and the people who served them was to an important extent a ceremonial relationship involving food, drink and festival. We lack many of the details of these activities, but it is clear that they were centralized under state control and were on a scale so massive and including so much space as to constitute the major focal point in the life of the city. Integration into the state was not merely a political, economic or military matter, but had an important underlying ritual significance. A center built for state administration accordingly provided large amounts of space as the setting for what was essentially a form of hospitality raised to the state level.

Modern states retain only dim reflections of these ceremonial aspects of administration. But in relatively early state societies, such as the Inca, representations of important parts of community ceremonial life often appear to have been maintained and even elaborated by the grander scale that increased resources and a larger organization made possible. At Huánuco Pampa traditional modes of sharing food and drink were probably used to cement loyalties and help motivate economic, political and military collaboration. They were the most direct and immediate ties between the state, as symbolized by the Inca or his governor, and the people – helping establish the notion that participation in the state was something more than working in the state's fields or fighting a distant war.

Production and the economics of administration

One of the primary activities that takes place in most urban centers is the production of non-agricultural goods. Manufacturing is an essential part of the economic base whereby a city traditionally acquires the subsistence goods it requires. It provides manufactured goods to rural areas that are part of the larger economic system in which it participates. Huánuco Pampa, however, seems not to have been a major manufacturing center. The limitations of the excavated sample have been pointed out, but still we doubt that we would have missed a major, quantitatively important, manufacturing activity. There are a couple of rock samples that may have been bores, and a few hints of very small-scale, almost incidental, production at the household level. The only evidence of production that was organized on a large scale and probably maintained on a full-time basis is the brewing of *chicha* and the production of textiles. The beer was brewed for consumption within the city as just described. In any case *chicha* does not store well, and it is unlikely that it was distributed in any meaningful quantity outside Huánuco Pampa.

Evidence for spinning and weaving in a small-scale household context occurs in most, but not all, parts of the site. In the Andean countryside today women spin as part of their daily activities, even when traveling. It is not surprising, therefore, to find small numbers of spindle whorls throughout much of the city. Bone tools used in weaving are also found sporadically. The only concentration of spinning and weaving tools is associated with the compound at the northern edge of the plaza described in the preceding chapter. As noted there, that compound also contained evidence of brewing, and we believe it to have housed a group of *aklla* women. The presence of domestic refuse certainly shows that people lived in at least most of the buildings of the compound, so it was not merely some sort of factory in which workers spent their days laboring away from home.

The use of *aklla* women for cloth production at Huánuco Pampa is still an hypothesis requiring further testing, but the evidence that the state had gone to some lengths to establish a facility for making cloth is apparent. Why does cloth making emerge as one of the principal activities in an administrative city like Huánuco Pampa? One might simply answer that cloth making is one of the main activities throughout the Andes, as is evident from the great wealth of textiles archaeologists find from all time periods. Cloth production centralized in a state-controlled city, however, would seem to have a special significance. John Murra has spelled out the unusual significance of cloth in the Andes,[40] observing how exchanges of cloth accompanied marriage and almost all the other important turning points in the life and death of an individual. He noted also that exchanges or gifts of cloth marked most important social and political events. The incorporation of groups newly conquered by military or diplomatic offensives into the empire, for example, was frequently marked by gifts of cloth. State service, particularly in the army, was similarly rewarded.

plate 9

Since cloth was such an important item of political as well as economic value, it is not surprising that the state took measures to assure itself of a substantial and growing supply. The more cloth it had, the more effectively it could raise and control armies and other workers, and the more successfully it could consolidate and control conquered areas. In other words, the growth of the state itself depended in part on its ability to increase and control the supply of textiles. Establishing a production facility under direct state control would obviously be a very effective means of insuring the supply of such an important commodity. Production of cloth at a center like Huánuco Pampa thus becomes an almost expected complement to its administrative functions. On the one hand cloth was a vital element in both the economic and political growth of the state, given the nature of the Andean economy. On the other hand such centers provided an ideal setting in which textile production could be controlled, increased and made in the standards and styles which symbolized the Inca and their state.

Labor taxes, state housing and the nature of residence

As we saw in the previous chapter, the material remains of Huánuco Pampa differ sharply from those of the local villages. While there are subtle similarities in some details, the imitation of Cuzco strongly suggests direct supervision of building and of ceramic manufacture to create an architecture and a ceramic assemblage identified with the state.

A reasonable interpretation of the marked distinction might be that the centers built by the state were isolated outposts, populated almost entirely by peoples transplanted from Cuzco, maintaining only the most minimal contact with the several ethnic groups in the surrounding region. However, the picture we get from the *visita* of Iñigo Ortiz does not portray so rigid and severe an isolation. There is little doubt that centers like Huánuco Pampa were identified with imperial pottery and were intrusive in relation to local groups and traditions. But this does not mean that they functioned as part of two separate worlds. On the contrary the *visita* shows that there was a regular movement of goods and people between Huánuco Pampa and local villages.

In Chapter 2 we mentioned the principles whereby the state controlled certain land and collected a labor tax. The Inca rulers claimed land and natural resources throughout *Tawantinsuyu*. The people of each region spent part of their time working the Inca's land and producing goods from his resources. Many of these goods were carried to the state centers where they were used or stored. But there was an even more direct inter-connection between the state center and the local villages than mere delivery of goods. The people were obliged to devote a portion of their time in service to the state. Such service followed several different forms of organization and involved such tasks as cultivating the state's fields or laboring in public construction projects. According to the Ortiz *visita*, some of the people from the surrounding region performed their labor service in Huánuco Pampa. Thus we know that this city which looks so intrusive and foreign was in fact built and occupied in large part by local people and supported economically by the harvests of the region. The élite which controlled it and supervised its construction were indeed outsiders, but the city had a regular and, from its point of view, very necessary relationship with its regional hinterland.

The differences between Huánuco Pampa and the villages of the Huánuco region were thus not the result of a lack of interaction, but rather the peculiar form interaction took. We are accustomed to a system or kind of urbanism based in great part on commerce and market activity. In such a system people from the countryside go rather freely into the urban center to trade their goods, leaving goods from the countryside and usually acquiring some of the products of other regions and perhaps of the city itself. If people from the countryside go to live in the city they typically carry many of their own possessions with them, and if they build houses they are likely to pattern them in part on what they were accustomed to in the countryside. The result brings considerable evidence of the urban contact to the countryside and a significant imprint of local goods and styles on the urban center.

We found no positive evidence of market activity in Huánuco Pampa, and our coverage of the city is sufficiently complete to suggest that no major spaces were given over to market style exchange. Products of the fields in the highly varied Andean landscape were exchanged instead among people related by kinship or political ties, and ordinarily these exchanges do not appear to have involved gathering at some common marketplace. Through such socio-political ties almost everyone had rights to goods in several different ecological zones. This clearly was a system which would have been subject to forms of economic and urban growth rather different from those with which we are most familiar. People came to Huánuca Pampa primarily because of their obligation to give service to the ruler, not for their economic betterment – although they almost certainly had access to certain goods and activities not available at home. The urban-rural interaction was thus not of a kind which encouraged unrestricted and casual interchange between village and city or which involved any significant amount of trade. It was a political phenomenon, controlled and in a sense compulsory.

The distinction between city and village we see in pottery and architecture may have been sharpened even further by a principle which can be gleaned from written records on Andean villages. People who labored on behalf of someone else, whether neighbor or chief, could expect to have their subsistence needs provided by the party for whom the work was done. If we can extend this principle from the community to the level of the empire, we can see how in state cities like Huánuco Pampa the government may have provided not just food but also housing – even housing furnished with ceramic vessels and other necessary household equipment. The cooking pots, plates and even buildings we find were created by the state in its own rather standardized style. The people who came to live and serve in the city had no need to bring their own things, since they knew they would be provided. And if they produced objects in the city as part of their work for the state, they would be done as the state wanted them, since they would be the property of the state, not that of the maker to be kept or traded. From all of this we can begin to understand the almost monotonous nature of material goods at Huánuco Pampa: they reflect fairly standardized state designs, virtual symbols of empire, not the rich variety we might expect in an urban center with a varied populace.

If the number of temporary labor taxpayers serving at Huánuco Pampa was large, we can see immediately that it would have affected the character of the administrative center. Cieza de León says that 30,000 people served the city,[41] but of course we have no way of knowing how many of these may have been there at any given time or whether he also included permanent residents. The whole question of the population is a very complex one, and so far we have no definite answers.

The sheer rapidity of the building and peopling of the city suggests large movements of people. Since it was founded on virgin soil, everyone was brought in – some from great distances. This implies both planning and powerful motivation to encourage people to move. The accomplishment becomes more comprehensible if a significant number of the houses were built for temporary residents spending only part of their time in Huánuco Pampa.

Some people were brought from Cuzco. But these were almost certainly a small minority. Most of the people who came to Huánuco Pampa came from local areas because of the Inca's ability to tap local sources of population. The institutions which gave the Inca access to people's labor and even to move them long distances for the purposes of the state are still not well understood, but at least three major categories of state personnel seem to have been involved. First is a group of retainers and other state functionaries who served the state on a continuous basis, and were supported by the state. The *aklla* was presumably such a group, and in an urban setting the members of these groups could be counted as essentially permanent residents. Many of them, however, like the *aklla*, did not live as family units. Instead they probably lived in some kind of communal housing, of which the compound discussed above is an example.

Second are the *mitmaq* colonists, who were moved in relatively large groups of ethnically and probably kin-related people. There is little positive evidence that such groups were moved into cities, but it certainly was a possibility. They would also presumably have been a relatively permanent group, and would probably have lived in family-type households.

Third are the best known of the state laborers, the temporary *mit'a* taxpayers. The *mit'a* was often served in agriculture, and did not involve long travel. But it was also used for construction and other public activities that could in part have taken place in centers like Huánuco Pampa. The *mit'a* was served in rotation, and it may have varied with the seasons. For example, people would probably not have been called upon to do construction or other tasks that would take them from the fields during peak agricultural seasons.

If these groups formed the base for the population of state cities, we can see immediately a picture that would be as complicated as it would be unusual. For example, if the *mit'a* formed a substantial part of the population there would not only have been rotation among the inhabitants as taxpayers served their terms and were replaced by others, but there may also have been significant seasonal variation in the number of inhabitants dictated by the agricultural cycle. The *mit'a* service was perhaps related to the ritual calendar in such a way that some of the religious and political ceremonies may also have been considered *mit'a*.

All these things are very difficult to test archaeologically. We are currently attempting a detailed study of the composition of the population through the patterns of use of Huánuco Pampa's buildings. There are clear differences in the size of buildings, layout, degree of planning, intensity of use, and other attributes which suggest differences in the social makeup of the residence unit. Particularly interesting is the distribution of artifacts which we tend to associate with women or female activities – such as spinning implements, the pins associated with women's garments and the distribution of culinary activities. In addition to the high concentration of women's artifacts we have already mentioned in the cloth-making facility, there are areas in which such artifacts are virtually absent. Cooking also does not seem to have been evenly distributed through the houses. These data, still being studied, imply that part of the population may have been segregated by sex, and that a very significant number of the inhabitants of the city lived almost dormitory style, being served from common kitchens.

This preliminary evidence seems to fit rather well the labor categories drawn from written sources and mentioned above. But we need to do additional work to get quantitative information on the number of inhabitants in the various categories if we are to have a meaningful profile of the population. At the moment we can only offer documentation that a wide range of living accommodation was available, and give a rough notion of the city's total housing capacity. We now guess that the city's buildings could have housed between 10,000 and 15,000 people.

The picture we have painted of Huánuco Pampa is in some senses a study in contradiction. On the one hand there is unquestioned evidence for specialized social and, to a lesser extent, economic groups. There are marked differences in rank and a well-organized system for making, communicating and enforcing decisions. Planning is elaborate and everywhere there is evidence of the power of the state to acquire the labor to construct and to turn natural resources into the goods it needed.

Yet if we are correct about the character of the population and the organization of production this large Inca center is really very different from our usual idea of the city, with its predominance of full-time resident specialists. We are less concerned with the semantic matter of whether or not Huánuco Pampa was a city than with documenting the activities that took place in it and the role it played in the larger system of which it was part. Two points at least are clear. First, it was part of a network of coordinated settlements, both within the region and over the empire as a whole. These settlements were dependent on each other in an extremely direct way, linked through socio-political organization not just trade. Second, it was indeed the locus of critical administrative functions. In a sense it was an elaborate stage set on which the rites which mediated between the state and its local populace occurred. Most of the activities we associate with administration were present – a decision-making élite, record keeping and logistical mechanisms for communication and the enforcement of the state's wishes. All of these, however, were covered by the ritual overlay of the principles which the Inca still used to mobilize people and goods. The nature of administration, and of the center, were shaped by the cultural context in which they occurred.

Many anthropologists would view this form of administrative city as marking a phase in an evolutionary sequence that would eventually culminate in something much closer to the bureaucratic, commercial cities with which we are more familiar. We tend to see it as a point on a relatively independent, though not necessarily unique, trajectory of development that resulted from local conditions and was continuing to develop along the lines charted through the centuries. Unfortunately we may never answer these questions fully; the fate of Huánuco Pampa and *Tawantinsuyu* was sealed by the invasion of 1532.

6 Subsistence and storage

The subsistence base of Huánuco Pampa lay some distance from the city itself. A small area adjacent to the northern periphery may have been under cultivation, but it could have supplied only a small proportion of the food necessary. Today the pampa produces potatoes exceptional in flavor, but not in large quantities. The altitude is simply too high for most other crops.

The source of the site's sustenance is clear:

. . . and that they tributed to him [the Inca] maize that they put in Huánuco Pampa; that it was that which was harvested in this valley (Huallaga) and from the fields of the Inca that they cultivated; and that they gave nothing from their own fields; and that it took them seven days to the storehouses from where they harvested it . . .; and that they tributed coca that they harvested in the *montaña* and they put it in nine days in the said Huánuco Pampa; and the fine cloth that they put half in Huánuco Pampa and the other half in Cuzco; and that in the same way they tributed salt and peppers and sandals and feathers from the *montaña* and they put them in the said Huánuco Pampa and the very good ones they took to Cuzco.[42]

These references to the regular transport of food and other products to Huánuco Pampa and other state centers are frequent in Iñigo Ortiz's interviews with the Chupaychu and the Yacha. Such groups at lower, more auspicious, altitudes for agriculture sustained Huánuco Pampa. Its provisionment was dependent on the coordination of a variety of lands and resources in a broad hinterland. Some of these lands and the groups that cultivated them are documented in Iñigo Ortiz, others are suggested by the ceramics found in several neighborhoods of the city of Huánuco Pampa, evidencing contact with various regions. The sustaining hinterland included at least the rich valleys of the Huallaga and the Marañón Rivers to the east and the Callejón de Huaylas to the west.

Dependence on such distant resources obviously provided a relatively fragile economic base. Besides the usual effects of weather fluctuations on crops, both production and delivery depended on a complex set of political motivations. Goods were not delivered to Huánuco Pampa to exchange in a market for other goods, but were the result of the populace fulfilling its labor obligations to the Inca. Of course those involved in production and delivery were the direct or indirect beneficiaries of some of the manufactures and ritual

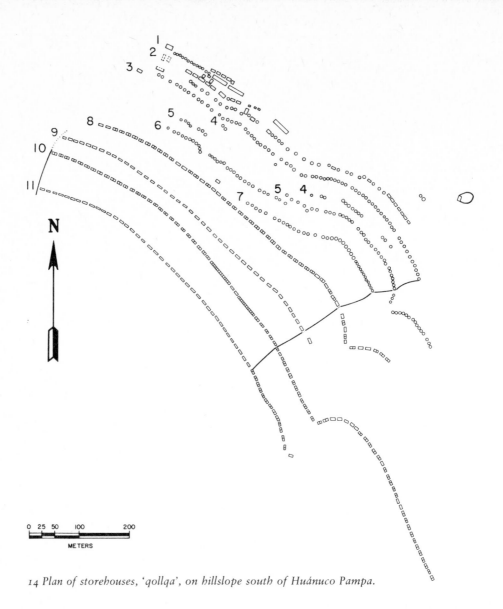

14 *Plan of storehouses, 'qollqa', on hillslope south of Huánuco Pampa.*

provided in the city as outlined in the previous chapters. But the strength of the bonds and the assurances that economic obligations would be fulfilled were essentially political, and not sufficiently secure to assure reliable operation of such a large installation in a marginal zone. Shifting alliances and rebellions were frequent problems throughout the Andes.

fig. 14
plates XIII, 22 The Inca solution to the problems of economic marginality and dependence on distant supplies is easy to determine. Long lines of storehouses overlook Huánuco Pampa from a hill to the south. Approaching the city on the Inca road from Quito and Cajamarca in the north one can see the warehouses from more than 30 km before actually reaching the city, announcing the wealth of the Inca and the security of his installation. The storehouses compensated for disjunctions between production or delivery and consumption needs –

*15 Guaman Poma drawing depicting Inca storehouses. A 'khipu'
official (right) relates accounting information to the Inca emperor (left).*

whether these arose because of normal seasonal variations, political
disruptions or a season of abnormal weather.

The fame of the Inca storage system goes back to the early European
observers. They were amazed at the incredible number of storage magazines *fig. 15*
and the great variety of goods they contained. The young Spanish soldier,
Pedro Cieza de León, writing less than twenty years after the fall of the Inca,
tells us:

. . . in more than 1,200 leagues of coast they ruled they have their representatives and
governors, and many lodgings and great storehouses filled with all necessary supplies.
This was to provide for their soldiers, for in one of these storehouses there were lances,
and in another, darts, and in others, sandals, and in others, the different arms they
employed. Likewise, certain buildings were filled with fine clothing, others, with

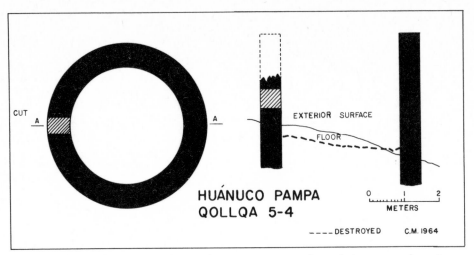

16 Plan of circular storehouse. The circular structures range from about 2 m to about 6 m in interior diameter. The most common diameter is about 5 m.

coarser garments, and others with food and every kind of victuals. When the lord was lodged in his dwellings and his soldiers garrisoned there, nothing, from the most important to the most trifling, but could be provided . . .[43]

The state warehouses of the Inca, at least in the Peruvian central highlands, have three primary identifying characteristics. Instead of regular doors with a threshhold at ground surface, they have one or more window-like openings. They are normally placed in rows on a hillside above any residential structures that may be associated with them. And, finally, in the excavated sample that had associated pottery, that pottery was overwhelmingly the large narrow-neck jar, commonly called 'aryballos' (our Form 1).

figs. 17, 16

The storehouses take two forms, rectangular and circular. The windows of circular structures face uphill. The rectangular *qollqa* of the top row and the third row from the top have a single room. Those of the second and fourth rows from the top are usually divided into two rooms, although this pattern is not entirely regular. Only two structures have more than two rooms.

From interior measurements and height approximations it is possible to calculate maximum volume capacities. The capacity of the circular storehouses at Huánuco Pampa was approximately 14,000 cubic m; the capacity of the zone of rectangular structures was almost 23,000 cubic m. Of course these maximum volume capacities are in excess of the quantities of any goods actually stored, since containerization and provision for air circulation consumed substantial space. The figures, nevertheless, assist comparisons of various parts of the Inca system and of Inca storage with warehousing arrangements of other times and places.

plate 53
plate 52

The excavation by Morris of a sample of ninety-five Huánuco Pampa *qollqa* had as its purpose the determination of stored goods, the methods of storage,

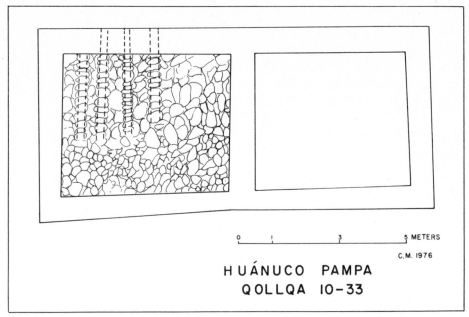

HUÁNUCO PAMPA
QOLLQA IO-33

17 Plan of rectangular storehouse. The length of single-room rectangular structures ranges from about 7 m to about 10 m, with a length of just over 9 m being most common.

and the uncovering of any architectural features associated with warehouses and storage technology that were not observable from surface remains. The results enable us to advance a series of hypotheses about storage methods and the functions of the various kinds of warehouses. Our sample of stored goods is not large and thus cannot be conclusive; furthermore, the results are not necessarily typical of storage practices elsewhere in the Inca realm.

As indicated in the quote from Cieza above, the early reports suggest that a broad range of products were stored by the Inca. The full spectrum of foods are included along with cloth, sandals and weapons. Exotic items such as dried birds are also mentioned.[44]

The uses to which the storehouses were put by the Inca is only one factor that affects what archaeologists find in them more than 400 years later. Preservation of botanical materials is poor in the rainy Andean highland environment. Plant products are usually preserved only when charred.

Historical factors also affect the nature of finds. In this case we must worry about the looting of storehouses or possible reuse of storage structures during the period following 1532. There is little evidence of reuse of Huánuco Pampa storehouses during the post-Columbian period. But wholesale removal of stored goods would certainly be expected. The large number of Inca storage vessels associated with areas of Spanish habitation were probably moved from the warehouses. It is also likely that all commodities were not equally affected. Goods such as cloth might have been looted more quickly and systematically – thus explaining the lack of any trace of them in the archaeological record.

Foods would more likely have been taken as needed. They are also more subject to spillage, and thus to leaving accidental traces. It appears that storehouses with religious significance or association were more likely to have been burned. So some of our clearest evidence comes from this context.

With these limitations of the data in mind, we can observe that substantial evidence was found for two categories of food: tubers and maize. The distribution of these products suggests both a pattern of internal specialization in the organization of the warehousing facility and an understanding of the technical requirements for storage of the two classes of foods.

The organization of the storehouses suggests that patterns of use varied in terms of the location of the storehouse or groups of storehouses within the facility. Since architectural variation is also related to storehouse position, a pattern of differing uses of the major architectural forms also emerges. The major variation seems to occur on an essentially vertical axis. Rows 1 and 2 at the bottom of the hill did not show a rigid pattern in either architectural arrangement (rectangular and circular structures are both present) or in the patterning of contents. It is not immediately apparent why this lower area is somewhat different. Morris has suggested two possibilities: 1. Goods were perhaps stored on a short-term basis for more immediate needs in this lower and more convenient position; 2. These lower stores may have been set aside for religious purposes. Some of the 16th-century sources tell us that the state's Sun religion had its own warehouses.[45] Structure 2–24 was not a storehouse at all, but a small shrine or other religious building. The circular *qollqa* flanking it appeared to have been dedicated to storage for it. It is even possible that both of these kinds of storage could have been carried out in the area; certain distinctions of architectural layout are noted between the eastern and western parts of the two rows.

Rows 3 to 11 seem more rigidly planned both in terms of their architecture and their apparent use. It should be noted that some of the complications of the arrangement in rows 4 and 5 are the results of topography and these rows could perhaps better be treated as a single row, in which case we would have four rows each of rectangular and circular storehouses. We feel that these structures housed the main bulk of long-term storage and that the two main sections of distinct building shapes were used differently.

plate 36

The main characteristics of the associations and distributions of foods found is that maize was found only in structures where ceramic jars also occurred. In two cases substantial quantities of shelled maize were actually found inside burned and broken jars. Tubers on the other hand were found between layers of straw derived from the common high-altitude Ichu grass, neatly bound with ropes into bale-like units. If the association of maize and pottery is valid then some of the limitations of the small sample of botanical remains are obviated and we have a better clue to storehouse use. Significant amounts of pottery were found in forty-three storehouses. All but five of these were circular. Three of the rectangular storehouses containing pottery were part of the small group at the eastern border of row 2. The lack of specialization in this part of the facility has just been indicated. Of the two examples of pottery associated with rectangular structures higher on the hill the ceramics may have intruded after the arrival of the Spanish in one case, and in the other the sherds were largely from vessels not in the typical storage form and their presence may have been incidental to the structures' primary storage function.

The storage of maize, at least in the shelled form we found, thus seems to be limited to circular structures. It is critical to point out that twenty-five circular buildings did not contain ceramics, and that in one case prepared charcoal was found in a well-preserved condition demonstrating that not all circular structures were reserved for maize. While only root crops were identified in rectangular *qollqa*, the sample is so small that we cannot conclude that rectangular storehouses were devoted exclusively to tubers; the specialized use of storehouses needs further testing with other data. But these results seem to suggest that at least partial internal specialization of storage was practiced. Except in special cases of storage related to shrines or, perhaps, limited short-term conditions, maize was stored shelled in jars in circular structures while tubers were kept in rectangular buildings. We strongly suspect, of course, that goods other than those we identified were stored at Huánuco Pampa. It is impossible to speculate, however, in what way their patterns of distribution might affect our picture of the organization of the warehouse facility. Internal organization of warehousing may have been based on more than simply providing a specialized storage for different products. Certain architectural features, particularly the walls of various lengths that run up and down the hill, partially segment the storage sector in an east-west direction. Our research was unable to determine what significance such divisions might have. We might expect storage to be arranged according to the groups that produced and delivered the goods – as a means of simplifying record keeping. Since all ceramic containers used were of the standardized variety produced for state purposes and probably not brought in with the goods, this hypothesis would be very difficult to test archaeologically. If variations assignable to minor ecological differences in the zones of production could be determined in the stored remains themselves, another avenue to studying the organization of the warehouses would be available, but such a test would require both extremely rich archaeological remains and good comparative collections from the zones in question; neither of these was present here.

In summary, a rather complex scheme of organization is suggested. In the vertical dimension, from the bottom of the hill to the top, maize may have been stored in circular structures lower on the hill and tubers in rectangular buildings higher up. This implies a vertical placement mirroring the respective positions of the crops in the vertical Andean ecology. Structures with certain religious association were given a special place, and some of the storehouses at the very bottom of the hill might have been used for short-term storage.

Possible east-west divisions across the hill, cross-cutting the vertical division, are topics for further exploration.

We have no written explanations of Inca storage technology in the words of an Inca official, but the material remains attest to a remarkable understanding of the storage requirements of the available foods and effective solutions to the problems they posed. The storage of maize, like that of other grains, is relatively simple. It is basically a matter of avoiding excesses of heat or humidity and isolating the grain from insects and rodents. The Andean root crops posed far more serious problems. The storage of tubers appears to have been particularly sophisticated, not really being surpassed until well into the present century when powered ventilation fans and refrigeration were introduced to control temperature. Unlike grains, tubers do not naturally lie dormant for long periods of time. They contain sufficient moisture for germination and tend to sprout if kept at a certain temperature for a long enough period of time. The high moisture content also makes them susceptible to a large number of bacterial and fungal infections, particularly if the skin is broken. In addition, chemical and structural changes may take place during storage which affect the taste of tubers. It is thus difficult to store potatoes and other root crops for even a few months, and truly long-term storage is impossible without some form of pre-storage processing which in effect converts the tubers to another substance.

The Inca solutions to the problems of tuber storage almost certainly rested on long experience and were not inventions of the Inca themselves, although they carried them to a scale of sophistication not previously evident. Two distinct approaches were used. One was to remove the moisture from the tubers by alternately freezing and drying them. The highly modified product which resulted was known as *chuño*.[46] The process takes admirable advantage of the warm days and cool nights in the Andean *altiplano* and the period following the harvest. The resulting *chuño*, if kept dry and protected from pests, is storable almost indefinitely. The identified remains of tubers found in the Huánuco Pampa storehouses had not been processed into *chuño*. The sample may once again be a factor, but the emphasis appears to have been on the unprocessed and therefore more difficult to store form.

The basic approach of the Inca at Huánuco Pampa appears to have been control of storage temperature by manipulating three factors in the storage environment: ventilation, insulation, and the selection of propitious locations for warehouses.

A temperature of about 3°C is required to keep potatoes completely latent; at about 4.5°C they sprout very slowly, but temperatures above 4.5°C can be tolerated for only a very few months. A complicating factor is that temperatures below 7°C cause some of the starch to be converted to sugar, affecting taste.[47] This side effect is partially reversible, but is nevertheless best avoided by storing the products at as high a temperature as possible while still suppressing sprouting. The optimum temperature on present evidence would

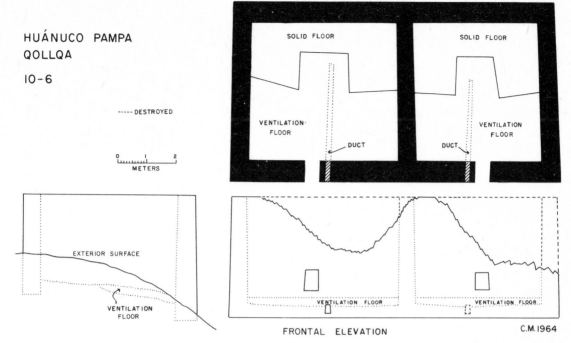

----- DESTROYED

0   1   2
METERS

SOLID FLOOR   SOLID FLOOR

VENTILATION   VENTILATION
FLOOR   FLOOR

DUCT   DUCT

EXTERIOR SURFACE

VENTILATION
FLOOR

VENTILATION FLOOR   VENTILATION FLOOR

FRONTAL ELEVATION   C.M. 1964

18 Plan of two-room rectangular storehouses. Note ducts in floors for ventilation.

seem to be about 4°C for most purposes. *Altiplano* environments similar to that at Huánuco Pampa have average yearly temperatures of about 3° to 6°C. This is obviously nearly ideal, assuming warehouse design can keep the storage temperature near the annual average. The point of departure for successful tuber storage at Huánuco Pampa is thus the use of the natural environment in or slightly above the zones in which most of the tubers are produced. The same areas that provide appropriate conditions for converting potatoes and other tubers into *chuño* also provide a natural refrigeration to suppress sprouting. The problem in using such zones for storage is thus less one of transporting the tubers from the fields where they were grown than of working out the complex relationships between storage and the locations of the people who maintain and use the storehouses. We have referred to the model of John Murra based on the strategy of Andean peoples to move populations into environments – often to take advantage of quite specific resources such as maizelands, pastures, cocalands, etc. Given this common, and apparently old, strategy, the use of cool environments for storage is not surprising. The organizational capability of a state familiar with such principles could easily not only move goods into advantageous storage environments, but could locate populations and activities dependent on stored food there as well. The prime storage conditions may have been a significant factor in selecting a site for the center that is, in terms of European notions of comfort, forbidding.

Ventilation and insulation were used by the Inca to moderate temperature extremes and approach the nearly optimum storage temperatures of the annual average provided by the climate. Given the tropical latitude, the oscillation between day and night is a more serious problem than the much less extreme seasonal variations. But these brief daily temperature extremes are also much easier to control.

The principles of temperature management in storehouses appear to have been relatively simple. The *qollqa* were provided with substantial walls and good thatched roofs to protect them during the warm days and prevent excessive cold. Ventilation was provided in the form of windows placed on both sides to provide cross-drafts and oriented so as to take advantage of the prevailing winds. Many rectangular storehouses also had open stone floors *fig. 18* connected by ducts or vents to the outside. Arrangement was made for opening and closing the floor ducts with stones. Several ducts were closed at the time of excavation. The windows or doors presumably could have been closed with cloth or some other material which was not preserved. While we have no descriptions of the operations of such a facility, it is likely that windows and floor vents were opened in the evening if internal temperatures rose, to take advantage of the cold outside air. It is interesting that in modern systems ventilation at the floor is especially effective in potato storage. The variety of ducts and floors in row 10 is such as to almost suggest experimentation with different kinds of floor ventilation. The construction of one of these systems suggests that it may have been designed to allow the addition of water to a sub-floor area below the surface on which stored items were placed. Humidity manipulation cannot be confirmed at Huánuco Pampa but, if used, it would have been fully effective as an additional temperature control as well as in alleviating the dehydration which damages tubers stored for long periods.

An expert on potato storage has suggested that all methods of potato storage are but compromises struck between a number of opposing requirements, and differences in practices may often have arisen because of a different emphasis placed upon these different requirements. It is the 'emphasis' that we have difficulty reconstructing for a people whose warehouses were involuntarily abandoned 450 years ago. However, the major requirements of successful root-crop storage now seem clear from modern situations; it is equally clear that the Inca understood these requirements and at Huánuco Pampa combined an impressive ingenuity in warehouse engineering with a deep understanding of the natural environments available to them.

We have said little specifically about the technology of maize storage. Our evidence that it was stored in jars suggests that it was adequately protected from rodents. It is difficult to say whether the practice of shelling is directly related to storage or whether it was simply done to make transportation more efficient, since in this case storage took place considerable distances from the zones of production. It also seems likely that maize storage at Huánuco Pampa has more to do with its need and use in the administrative center than it does with the advantageous storage conditions there. The cool *altiplano* temperatures are certainly helpful in controlling insects, as well as in most of the other potential problems of maize storage. However, the lower temperatures are not nearly as critical as they are for fresh tubers.

Storage and the support of state activities

In the theory of Louis Baudin that the Inca had a 'socialist empire' the role of the warehouses is to secure the welfare of the general populace by eliminating the hunger that might arise from occasional crop failures. As John Murra has pointed out, Baudin's theory erroneously assigns to the state functions of food supply that were largely fulfilled by local communities and polities. He suggests that the storehouses were involved in the commodity-exchange function of a redistributive state economy.[48] In such an economy the state presumably receives commodities as tribute, or in this case as a result of its labor tax. Some of these goods are used to maintain the state élite, the military and other personnel. Other goods are given out to the populace as gifts and issues, with the commodities received being different from those tributed or, in this case, produced in the state's fields or with the state's resources. One effect of such a system would be to 'redistribute' the products from one ecological zone to other different zones and the wares of specialists throughout the population. The state structure in this model essentially serves the functions of a market. The state warehouses handle the goods between receipt and their being dispensed to their ultimate users. The storage system is in a sense a substitute, physically, for a marketplace.[49]

Both the welfare-state theory and the redistribution, market-substitute theory imply the flow of significant quantities of goods out of the warehouses and into the hands of the common people. It is difficult to measure such a flow archaeologically when we are dealing mainly with perishable goods. As we shall see in the following chapters, in the Huánuco region there is little evidence for a substantial movement of goods from Huánuco Pampa into the hinterland villages we studied in the Huallaga Valley. To the extent that ceramics accompanied such movements, they were small and limited to particular political context. Furthermore, there is no indication in Iñigo Ortiz that significant quantities were brought out of Huánuco Pampa to local towns and villages. The traffic in goods seems to have been essentially one way: into the city. This may in part be the result of the Ortiz questionnaire. We would hardly expect the Spanish Colonial government to have drawn attention to services previously provided by the Inca government to its peoples. Nevertheless, had the local people actually been dependent on state warehouses for either their food or the exchange of goods between different zones and different specialists we would expect more evidence of it to have crept into the report of his inspection.

We feel that the distribution of the contents of Huánuco Pampa's huge stores is clear. Given the city's large size, its newly established and rather artificial character, and the marginality of food production at this altitude, Huánuco Pampa was dependent on the warehouses. They were a buffer against disjunctions in the delivery of food brought in from far away fields. They provided an important measure of security so that the ceremonial and logistical functions of the administrative center could be reliably discharged.

Of course in the normal functioning of the state center certain goods were redistributed to the people resident, visiting or serving there. Much of this redistribution came through the state's obligations to support its subjects while in service and undoubtedly took the form of the usual food, probably including lots of potatoes and other tubers if our suggestion regarding storehouse contents are correct. But there was also maize, and we have documented brewing as a major activity. John Murra has shown how maize was a special and prized product,[50] especially in the Andean highlands were its availability was restricted in most areas. Goods such as maize, beer and cloth were, thus, redistributed by the state in the sense that some people received different quantities of them than they would have received without the Inca's intervention. To a large extent the redistributed goods were consumed on the spot and to the direct benefit of the state.

It is even possible that the storehouses functioning in a system of urban supply could be pressed into relief service in the event of famine. Besides the possible occasional emptying of the magazines to prevent spoilage, given the pattern of rotating residence we have suggested, we might speculate that areas with food shortages had a greater percentage of their population shifted into the state's centers, or the time their people spent in such centers increased. Support could have thus come from the state's reserves.

Many of the questions of the use and economic role of stored wealth obviously require quantitative information on the complete cycle of movement of goods from point of production through storage to point and context of consumption. Acquiring this information from archaeological data is possible, as we have seen here, but it is difficult because of the quantity of material and the wide areas and broad contexts that must be studied.

Even without as much economic data as we would like, we can see the storage-based subsistence system was in keeping with the overall character of Huánuco Pampa as a state-built and -supported center with primarily political functions. To a certain extent goods were moved from one area of context to another, but the economy was mainly concerned with maintaining the center itself and its political and ritual activities. The emphasis was on a kind of political mobilization in which goods were accumulated and invested in the growth of the state and the state's economy. Financing the ceremonies at the core of administration and political growth in a system based on feasting and gift giving seems to have been the aim of the impressive storage facility. In a manner similar to the cloth-production facilities, valuable goods were transferred to a context where they could stimulate continuing political – and thereby economic – growth.

7 Roads, bridges and waystations: the infrastructure of Inca rule in the provinces

The Inca highway

Aside from the Inca administrative center of Huánuco Pampa itself, the most obvious indication of the Inca presence in the Huánuco area is the famous Inca highway and its associated *tampu* or waystations and other wayside buildings. The importance of the road to Inca expansion and rule has been repeatedly stressed. Clearly the road could be used to move troops rapidly to wherever they were needed. Similarly, it could also function both as a military supply line and as a route for moving other goods to their destinations. The *visita* speaks of goods being carried southward as far as Cuzco itself, and occasionally northward to Tumebamba and Quito in Ecuador. Presumably the Inca highway was the path along which they were moved. Indeed the Inca emperor himself upon occasion was carried along the road in his royal litter, presumably in a manner similar to his entrance to Cajamarca described in Chapter 1, and many lesser state dignitaries no doubt used it in the course of their official duties.

Equally important, the road functioned in the transmission of information of state concern, an essential operation in the running of so vast an empire. Numerous writers from the Colonial period and later comment on the *chaski* or relay runner who forwarded messages along the road between fairly closely spaced stations. The *chaski* system was apparently very efficient, and one suspects that the messages were seldom purely verbal, but rather were accompanied by a *khipu*, a mnemonic device of cords knotted in a positional decimal system. Otherwise the information could easily have become distorted either by accident or by design.

There is also some evidence that the system functioned in other ways as well; along another route, for example, fresh fish was supposed to have been rushed from the Pacific coast to the emperor's table in highland Cuzco. It would appear that there is nothing new in making personal use of state facilities.

In the course of our work we followed the Inca road south of Huánuco Pampa to the *tampu* of Tunsucancha and north of Huánuco Pampa to the *tampu* of Taparaku. Recently John Hyslop has restudied the section between Huánuco Pampa and Tunsucancha in greater detail.[51]

The first European to describe this section of the road was Miguel de Estete, who accompanied Hernando Pizarro on a trip to the coastal shrine of Pachacamac while Francisco Pizarro and the remaining Spaniards held the Inca Atahualpa captive in Cajamarca. The description is of the return journey in March 1533.[52]

The following day they went on to pass the night at another town called Tonsucancha, the chief of which is called Tallima; and here they were well received, and there were many people serving there, because, although the town was small, the people from the surrounding area had gathered there to receive and to see the Christians. In this town there are many small animals which have very fine wool, like the wool of Spain. The following day they went on to spend the night at another town called Guaneso [Huánuco Pampa], which was five leagues away by road, the better part of which was paved and flagstoned and provided with drains to let the water pass. They say it was made in this fashion because of the snows which fall in this country at certain times of year.

On the last day of the above mentioned month, the captain [Hernando Pizarro] departed with his companions from this town [Guaneso] and they arrived at a bridge [the bridge of Huánuco Viejo] over a torrential river, made of very thick timbers, and at it there were gatekeepers who had charge of collecting the toll, as is the custom among these people. This day they went on to sleep at a town four leagues away [probably Taparaku] where Chilicuchima took care of all their needs for that night.

The road as we observed it on foot and on horseback is a remarkable piece of engineering. Depending on the terrain, the road may vary in width from 3 to 15 m, steep sections tending to be narrow, flat ones, wide. When skirting across slopes, as it is on much of its way, it is leveled through the use of a stone masonry retaining wall on the downhill side.[53]

Much of the road is paved, especially in marshy areas, and open drains frequently cross it to prevent flooding. Steadily flowing streams sometimes pass under the road in closed culverts. Where the road ascends slopes, masonry steps are frequently used, sometimes zigzagging in a series of switchbacks. Often on gentle slopes the steps are staggered with a few steps being set between flat or slightly sloping sections.

plate 55

plate 58

The *tampu* of Tunsucancha

fig. 19

plate 54

The *tampu* of Tunsucancha lay on the southernmost section of the road that we surveyed south of Huánuco Pampa. The best-preserved section of Tunsucancha consists of a rectangular enclosure at the extreme west end of the site, overlooking a marsh. The enclosure is divided into three sections containing a total of ten or eleven rectangular structures. All the buildings are of typically Inca rectangular proportions, and one of them preserves a good Inca-style trapezoidal doorway and several trapezoidal niches.[54]

Excavations in a building designated A, at the northeast corner of the enclosure, yielded post-Conquest cattle bones in the top level of 50 cm. Below

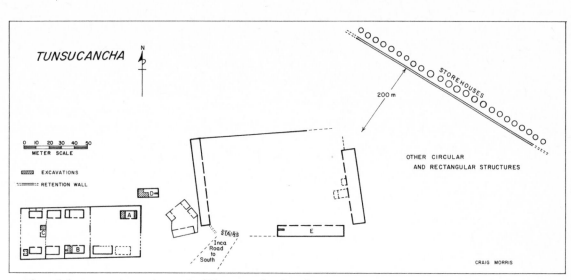

19 *Plan of the waystation or 'tampu' of Tunsucancha. See plate 54.*

this, however, was a floor with a thin (2–5 cm) level of scorched earth and ash on top of it, strongly suggesting that the house had burned. Mixed with this level of ash were fragments of bone and pottery, including sherds of Inca polychrome wares. The west end of the structure was divided off into a small room by a cross wall, though the place of entry into the small room remains uncertain, perhaps because of high door sills. Excavations in this small room revealed great quantities of ash, mostly domestic pottery, in contrast to the polychrome in the other room, and a semicircle of stones. We reached the tentative conclusion that the west room served as the kitchen for a house in which a rather important person had lived, as indicated both by the presence of the polychrome pottery and the location of the house within the compound.

Building B was located in the southeast corner of the central section of the enclosure. Excavations here yielded much less material and no evidence of cooking. While it still seems likely that the structure was residential in function, the occupation was probably shorter or more sporadic.

Building C, located in the center of the east wall of the westernmost section of the enclosure, was the best preserved of all. Moreover, it was the only building whose long axis ran north-south. In addition, it clearly preserved evidence of at least two trapezoidal niches and a trapezoidal doorway, all hallmarks of Inca architecture. On the other hand, it yielded little pottery, suggesting that it functioned as a domestic structure rarely, if ever.

The enclosure as a whole invites comparison with the eastern section of Huánuco Pampa, the 'casa del Inca,' discussed in earlier chapters. The two complexes share a tripartite division, a view overlooking water, masonry superior to most of the rest of the site, and orientation to the cardinal points. This comparison would gain added strength if the small structure in the southwest corner of the Tunsucancha compound were to prove upon excavation to be a bath, as it appears to be on the surface. Such baths are typical of the ceremonial sections of all major Inca sites, including the eastern section of Huánuco Pampa. Like that group of buildings, the Tunsucancha compound may have functioned as a combination of royal apartment and ceremonial complex.

Building D was the designation given to a small, isolated, rectangular structure lying off the northeast corner of the western compound, described above. Like some of the structures in the western compound, the quantity of ash found in the excavation suggested that the building had been burnt. Building D, however, was unusual in that it had a small low platform at the west end and contained charred botanical materials and large quantities of pottery, all concentrated at that end. The pottery, which included many plates, did not appear to be domestic kitchen ware, though two vessels contained food remains. On the basis of the evidence of the platform, food remains and non-domestic pottery, we tentatively assume that the building served some sort of religious or ceremonial purpose, perhaps in connection with offerings made by travelers stopping at the *tampu*.

To the east of structure D lies the main plaza of Tunsucancha, flanked on its south, east and west sides by long buildings called *kallanka* and on the north by a long wall. Short walls supplement the *kallanka* to complete the enclosure. The Inca highway enters and exits through the northeast and southwest corners of the plaza. The arrangement suggests a miniature version of the great plaza at Huánuco Pampa, which had similar long buildings on some of its sides. Tunsucancha, however, lacks the central platform or *ushnu* found at Huánuco Pampa and at other major sites.

A trench excavated at the west end of the southern *kallanka*, called building E, yielded little pottery, but the area of excavation was so small in relation to the size of the building that it cannot be considered as representative. This *kallanka* and those to the east and west very likely functioned like those at Huánuco Pampa discussed above.

East of the plaza lay a badly disturbed zone of circular and rectangular structures that probably served for low-status housing, as the excavation of one circular house suggested. This area could not be mapped in the time available, but probably corresponded to the outlying districts of Huánuco Pampa in function. It is very likely that a rotating population of people who served at Tunsucancha lived there for predetermined lengths of time as part of their service to the state. Precisely such service is referred to in the testimony of Juan Chuchuyauri, chief of the Yacha, in the *visita* of Iñigo Ortiz.

Northeast of the plaza on a nearby hillside a row of twenty-four circular structures had been constructed. These were certainly storehouses or *qollqa* to judge by comparisons with other storage areas such as that at Huánuco Pampa. The *qollqa* at Tunsucancha averaged about 3.5 m in diameter, a size at the small end of the range of these structures at Huánuco Pampa. The walls were badly fallen. But assuming a mean height of about 3.3 m, the equivalent of that found at Huánuco Pampa, where preservation was better, then the row would have had a total storage capacity of about 390 cubic m. This is only a tiny fraction of the some 30,000 cubic m at Huánuco Pampa, but probably enough to maintain the site.

Presumably the goods stored in the warehouses were used to run the *tampu* and to feed official travelers or a passing army. What we do not fully understand is the system of supplying the storehouses. Were goods deposited directly in Tunsucancha or were they routed through an administrative center such as Huánuco Pampa to the north or Pumpu to the south? The storage may not have been large enough to warrant a full-time accountant, and there do not seem to have been any administrative buildings associated with the storage as there are at Huánuco Pampa. Presumably, however, the administration could have been handled by a part time specialist.

As we have already pointed out, Tunsucancha contains many details reminiscent of Huánuco Pampa, and this fact raises many questions. As far as function is concerned, was Tunsucancha just a waystation where people on state business spent the night, or was it a kind of minor center where events of a local nature also took place under the direction of a permanent minor official or during the visits of more important officials? It appears to be a very elaborate site to have served only as a wayside inn. The image of its being a focal point of Inca administration with occasional major events associated with high-ranking officials in transit is an appealing one, especially in the light of Miguel de Estete's description quoted above. Such interpretation brings to mind the way remote villages today turn out for the occasional visit of a government official or the visit of a priest for the annual fiesta.

From Tunsucancha to Huánuco Pampa

On the basis of the distance between Tunsucancha and Huánuco Pampa there was probably at least one more *tampu* in Inca times. John Hyslop has recently identified a site called Tamborajra as a likely candidate for the intervening *tampu*. He has also made the interesting suggestion that *tampu* are sometimes omitted from the Colonial-period lists because the speed of travel, hence the daily distance covered, increased with the introduction of horses. As a result, a number of *tampu* were regularly bypassed and abandoned soon after the Conquest. Hyslop describes Tamborajra as similar to Tunsucancha in many respects, including the presence of long structures resembling *kallanka*. He also describes several other sites associated with the road which were probably not *tampu*, though what function they did serve is unknown.[55]

We did not visit Tamborajra or the other sites that Hyslop describes with the exception of one called today Pueblo Viejo or sometimes Caliente. Pueblo Viejo lies beside the Inca highway close to the Nupe River, near the modern town of Baños, which takes its name from the bath at Pueblo Viejo.[56]

Most of the walls at Pueblo Viejo have been destroyed by cultivation, but by careful observation it is possible to deduce that quite a large site once existed there over an area somewhat greater than 300 × 400 m. One fairly clear feature is a plaza over 50 m square with a long building rather like a *kallanka* along its west side. Since we were unable to confirm any details of the structure by excavation there are problems about its form, date and function. Some of the local people refer to the ruined building as *iglesia* and *capilla*, words meaning 'church' in Spanish. It is thus possible that it is a ruined Colonial-period church, rather like one that we excavated at the Chupaychu site of Ichu, to be discussed in Chapter 8. Or, more likely, it may have been a *kallanka* modified in the Colonial period to serve as a church and was so used until the town was moved to the site of modern Baños. There are indications of at least one other similar long building on the other side of the plaza, confirming the likelihood that several *kallanka* were present, rather than one church.

In addition to the plaza and possible *kallanka*, there is a bridge foundation where the Inca road crosses the Nupe River. Unfortunately the corresponding foundation on the other side has been destroyed by the meandering river, but the road can be seen ascending the slope on that side of the valley.

All around the area are fragments of stone foundations, some of which appear to outline structures. The presence of additional former walls was also indicated in lines of lighter green in a field of alfalfa. No finely cut stone remains at Pueblo Viejo except at the bath to be described below, but well-cut stone blocks are found in local house foundations and in the foundations of the church in nearby Baños. Local informants specifically stated that the site had been robbed for such stone.

fig. 20
plate 57

The most interesting feature at the site was the bath which had been built and paved with cut stone and is still in quite good condition. The walls are clearly Inca and even contain the remains of niches. The bath measures 5 × 7 m and is divided in half by a meter-wide wall. It is fed by a hot spring which is channeled into the bath and drains out the other side to the nearby Nupe River. The bath is in such good condition that it is still occasionally used by residents of Baños, some 5 km away.

Pueblo Viejo is not in a sufficiently good state of repair to discuss in any detail. It has some typical Inca features such as plaza, bath, *kallanka* and proximity to the highway, but it differs from most of the rest of the Inca sites in Huánuco in its setting in a temperate valley. We believe that the Inca tended to prefer to locate their sites in the high altitude grasslands in order to provide good pasture for their herds of llamas. Pueblo Viejo is an exception in this regard. Perhaps the hot water was too great a gift to ignore; perhaps the site had a somewhat different function from the *tampu* and administrative centers. Was it a resort? Without additional work we cannot be sure.

One last point should be made with regard to this section of the highway south of Huánuco Pampa. John Hyslop has described a site which he has named Sirrom. It is located on the highway at the point where one first catches

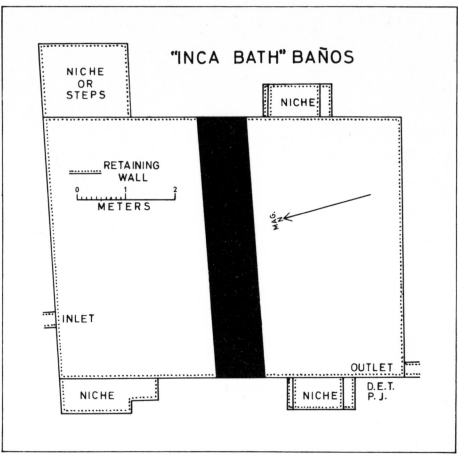

20 *Plan of the Inca bath at Baños. The central wall is an unusual feature of uncertain function. See plate 57.*

sight of Huánuco Pampa. Whether it performed a ritual or a practical function we do not know, but sites with similar locations are known from elsewhere on the road.[57]

The bridge of Huánuco Viejo to Taparaku

From Huánuco Pampa the road continues northward, descending almost at once to the Vizcarra River, formally known as the Urqumayu, which it crosses by means of a log bridge called the bridge of Huánuco Viejo. It then ascends again by means of a long switchbacked staircase to continue northward to the next *tampu*.

    The bridge of Huánuco Viejo was the center of some Colonial-period litigation, and, as a result, we have some unique documentary information on how it was constructed. Moreover, it appears as though the bridge was

plate 58

plate 56

maintained through the intervening centuries and as a result looked – until its recent destruction in a flood – much as it did in Inca times, though smaller.[58]

Because a local town brought a lawsuit to the Lima courts over the question of who should be responsible for maintaining the bridge, an official inspector by the name of Diego de Espinoza Campos was sent out to investigate the problem in 1596. He inspected a number of local bridges and took down testimony on how the bridges had been maintained. He described the bridge of Huánuco Viejo in the following way:[59]

I walked from one side of the bridge to the other and I saw the abutments of it, which appear to have been securely and very well made in the time of the Inca, and so far as one can see they are permanent from being well finished, and [I] measured the said bridge and its timbers with a rope and a *vara* [a measure, approximately a yard] sealed with the seal of the city of Huánuco, and I counted the timbers and *canes* of it [canes are supports for the bridge which project slightly over the river from the abutments].

The timbers of the bridge: there are 7 logs [each of which] a man could enfold by stretching both arms around them; these cross the river from one side to the other over the *canes*. The 2 in the lower position are broken, and the 5 which are whole, or seem to be seen from below, were measured with the rope and *vara*. They are $17\frac{3}{4}$ *varas* because they rest on top of all the *canes* and they are recessed into the wall; the bed of the river from wall to wall is 15 *varas* and 4 inches.

The timbers of the *canes*: on both sides it has 3 tiers of thick beams, 5 beams in each tier. The tier in which the ends of the beams were most readily visible, and which they say are of the same size as all the rest, were each 6 *varas* long. Of these [6] *varas*, 4 penetrate into the wall, and the *canes* project 2 *varas* over the river, and this totals 30 thick timbers of 6 *varas* each.

The timbers which they place over the *canes*: there are more than 6 thick logs which cross over the *canes*, 3 on either side of $2\frac{1}{3}$ *varas* each and this is the width of the bridge, of the 7 said timbers, which rest on the *canes* and which make up the said bridge.

plate 56   The bridge in recent times was very much the same, though not as wide and with fewer supports. The foundations of the modern bridge were built of both cut stone blocks and rough fieldstone, and we suspect that although there was probably some rebuilding, the foundations were essentially the same as in Inca times, especially toward the bottom.

The modern bridge spanned a distance of 11.2 m between the two foundations. As in the Colonial period, the main logs were supported on *canes*, though with only 2 tiers of 3 logs each as opposed to the 3 tiers of 5 logs each in the Colonial period. Three main logs spanned the river instead of the 7 described by Espinoza Campos.

In addition to the physical description of the bridge, Espinoza Campos also describes the division of labor employed in bridge construction. This involved the social divisions of *allauca* and *ichoc* (right and left). As Espinoza Campos was told: 'The river separated them; those of Allauca Guanuco were on the side toward Huánuco Viejo [the right side looking downstream] and those of Ichoc Guanuco on the side of the river where the Tambo of Taparaku [the next *tampu* north, to be discussed below] is located . . .' It is apparent from the text that the work on the bridge was evenly shared between the villages on the right and left sides of the river. The job of providing the logs for the bridge was specifically allocated, log by log, to the villages on the two sides. This was an important matter, since such big logs were difficult to obtain at this high altitude. Indeed, it was over the matter of providing the logs that the litigation was initiated in the first place.

The *allauca-ichoc* division is a system that antedates the Inca in this area and is referred to in the chronicle of Guaman Poma, who is believed to have come from the Huánuco region. The Inca system, by contrast, is based on an upper-lower division (*hanansaya-urinsaya*) and is found in Huánuco only in Inca-founded towns, usually *mitmaq* ones. In remote villages a modified version of the old local *allauca-ichoc* division still survives today in the context of the religious fiesta system.

The bridge of Huánuco Viejo, then, was until recently much the same as it was 450 years ago, a living remnant of the Inca period. Unfortunately, it was destroyed in the floods of 1980 and the old social divisions are disappearing under the impact of modern technology and social change. Salvage ethnography may thus be as important for the understanding of future archaeology and ethnohistory as it is for cultural anthropology.

The road continues northward from the bridge to the next *tampu*, called Taparaku, a Quechua word meaning big butterfly.[60] It is a large site which plate 51 contains plazas flanked by long buildings similar to *kallanka*. The best-preserved building is a long rectangular enclosure containing nine pairs of rooms built on either side of a central passageway. This building in no way resembles the rectangular enclosure at Tunsucancha. The plazas and long buildings, however, are common to both sites, and there are other badly fallen structures at Taparaku which could have fulfilled the function of the western enclosure at Tunsucancha. The site has been severely disturbed by modern corral building, but at least seventy-three rectangular and circular houses were visible. One problem was the apparent lack of storage facilities. Subsequent examination of air photographs of the *tampu* showed a possible line of structures on the other side of a hill, out of sight of the immediate area we were surveying. Tentatively we are considering this as a possible storage area.

The construction at Taparaku was of rough but fairly well-fitted stone. There was no finely cut stone visible on the surface. The pottery collected was clearly Inca derived. Unfortunately, the site has been dismantled to make modern houses and corrals and, except for the main plazas and the north enclosure, it is difficult to map and to interpret.

Some concluding comments

Huánuco Pampa, then, stands as a major Inca administrative center along a stretch of the royal road which contains other imperial installations, notably *tampu*, but also bridges, baths and other structures of undetermined function.

The construction and maintenance of the road was the responsibility of the local people and, in the case of the bridge at least, was clearly divided on the basis of the pre-existing social organization, a policy the Inca apparently followed regularly. The exact way in which the labor was mobilized to build the road itself and the associated *tampu* we do not yet know for certain, but we can probably safely assume that a similar system prevailed. The *visita* of Iñigo Ortiz clearly indicates that members of the local Yacha ethnic group served at Tunsucancha, and we can probably assume that nearby Wamalis or others served at Taparaku, though we have no documentary support for such an assumption so far.

Finally, it seems clear that the whole road system with its paving, stairs, elaborate drains, culverts, bridges and *tampu* was far more elaborate than purely physical needs would require. The road system was probably as much symbolic as it was practical; such an elaborate road was probably not necessary even to move armies. It was, however, an outward and visible sign of the Inca presence and sovereignty, a constant reminder of Inca rule. The local peasants, moreover, were responsible for building and maintaining this symbol of the Inca presence in their lands; yet they were probably not even allowed to use it except on officially sanctioned occasions. One can thus imagine that for the Inca it was a familiar artifact, which linked together the highly varied segments of the empire. For the conquered peoples, on the other hand, it was a symbolic thorn in the side, a constant reminder of their subservience to Cuzco, which lay far to the south on the same road, as some of them knew who had carried goods there.

8 The Chupaychu ethnicity

Our archaeological study of the Chupaychu began with a survey in the area of Huánuco known as Pachitea Andina on the right bank of the Huallaga (Pillkomayu) River, downstream from modern Huánuco. We surveyed five villages, three of which were later tested by excavation. Three sites were visited in the initial survey: Paco, which we subsequently tested and will be discussed later, Watuna, and Quero.

fig. 4

Watuna (Guatuna – also called Chaquiposo today) is almost certainly the Guatana described in the *visita* of 1549 as having 17 houses in which lived 16 men, 12 widows and 6 unmarried girls. The headman was named Macori and he, in turn, was under the Cacique, Querin. By 1562 Macori had been replaced by one Sabastian Mallu, but, since the village was not actually visited by Iñigo Ortiz, we have no comparative house or population figures.[61]

The houses at the site of Watuna appear to be clustered in small, irregularly arranged groups along a low ridge. The position is not as defendable as that found at some of the other villages located in the more sharply dissected terrain closer to the major watercourses. It is difficult to estimate the number of houses without clearing and excavation, but fifteen to thirty would probably be a safe figure, based on both our estimates. In the cases where the foundations could be clearly observed, the houses were almost perfectly square in plan with rounded interior corners and with a gabled roof supported by masonry end walls. The masonry itself was rather crude, consisting of rough angular stone set in mud mortar – what is locally called *pirka*. Some of the walls contained small irregular niches.

Quero, which also lies on a rounded ridge crest, had very similar houses, square in plan with rounded interior corners and gabled roofs. In several cases the door was clearly visible in one of the gabled ends. The best preserved of the houses also retained a horizontal line of irregular niches under one of the masonry gables, a feature subsequently found in other houses at other Chupaychu sites. It is possible that the irregular niches served as sockets for the beams of a floor under the pitched roof. Such attics may be seen in contemporary Indian houses, where they serve as storage areas. Today, these ancient niches are sometimes reused by the local Indians, who place in them offerings of tobacco, rum and coca leaves to the *Awkillos* or Ancient Ones.

plate 60

At least one of the structures at Quero had an interior dividing wall. As at

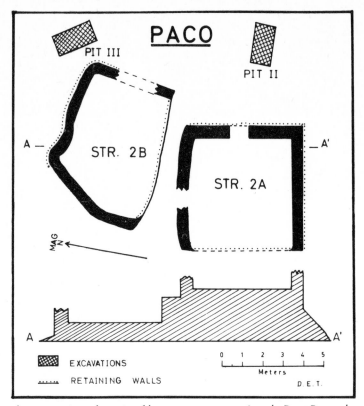

21 *Plan and cross-section of a pair of houses, structures 2A and 2B, at Paco, showing how the ideal square shape can be distorted by the terrain and how side-by-side houses can be on different levels with walls serving partly retaining functions.*

Watuna, the houses appear to be in small groups along the ridge. Some of the groups gave the impression of having been an arrangement of houses around an open space, but this kind of formal ordering was neither consistent nor obvious. One is tempted, of course, to think in terms of extended family groupings, which brings up the interesting question of whether a *visitador* defined a house as a single structure for one or more persons or as a house group for an extended family.

The *visita* of 1549 records 16 houses at Quero in which lived 10 Indians and 2 widows. The headman was named Naopa and the *cacique* or leader, Quixuy. The villagers were carpenters by trade, according to the *visita*.

The site of Paco was chosen for limited excavation, along with Warpo, a nearby village first surveyed during the work at Paco. The *visita* of 1549 refers to Paco as Pacon and reports from there 24 houses in which there dwelled 14 Indians and 6 widows. The *cacique* and headman are not recorded, though the latter may well have been Paria Vilca, who was in charge of several neighboring communities. In 1562 the headman was Domingo Sangao, but we have no additional information on the village from that date.

Huánuco Pampa ceramics

35 Large polychrome jar from Cuzco, commonly and inappropriately called an 'aryballus', and similar to Form 1 at Huánuco Pampa (plate 36).

36 A large jar (Form 1), with a narrow neck and pointed base, from Huánuco Pampa. Excavated from a storehouse, the jar contained shelled maize.

37 A variant of the Form 1 jar.

38 A clay support for the Form 1 jar; the pointed bottom of the jar rested in the hole in the center.

39 A large wide-mouth jar (Form 3) *in situ* against the wall of a house.

40 A stack of Inca plates *in situ* (Zone II, B2) on the floor of a building in the eastern sector.

41 Cat faces and a human face on modeled pottery fragments.

42 Bone weaving implements found inside a compound where cloth was produced.

43 Spindle whorls are evidence for spinning at Huánuco Pampa.

44 A bronze pin found in Zone V, B with a llama head at the top.

Ritual and ceremony

45, 46 The floor of a small building in a residential area of the southern part (Zone III, C) of the city. The small circular stone near the center (*above*) covered a tube filled with small stones leading to an underground stone-lined reservoir (*below*). The architecture and location of this structure suggest it was of ritual use, related to the common residents of the city rather than state ceremonies. Two large grinding stones were placed in a seat-like arrangement in the chamber and human bones were found on the horizontal stone.

47 This Inca 'bath' (*opposite, above*), is part of the waterworks in the ceremonial eastern sector (Zone II, B) of Huánuco Pampa.

48 A bone flute (*opposite, center*). Music was a common part of ritual.

49 A cache of Inca pots *in situ* (*opposite, below left*), found under the threshold at the entrance to a large building associated with feasting in the eastern sector.

50 A large fragment of a wooden drinking vessel, a *kero* (*opposite, right*), was preserved in Huánuco Pampa's moist soil because it was carbonized (Zone II, B2).

Huánuco Pampa storehouses

52 A square storehouse at Huánuco Pampa.

53 A round storehouse at Huánuco Pampa. Cf. plate 22.

Inca waystations

51 The waystation (*tampu*) of Taparaku. There is a long building containing rooms in the center of the picture and a plaza flanked by long halls (*kallanka*) below. Some of the construction could have been done by local peasants making corrals after the abandonment of the site.

54 Western section of the waystation of Tunsucancha. See *fig. 19*.

On the Inca highway

55 The Inca highway. Quite wide here, it is buttressed by a retaining wall on the downhill side. An open stone-lined drain channels water runoff across it.

56 The bridge of Huánuco Viejo, appearing here almost exactly as it did in Inca times. A Spanish expedition crossed and described it in 1533 and later it became the center of an important legal investigation. Floods destroyed it in 1980.

57 Inca bath at Baños, viewed from the north. Local people still use the bath, which has natural hot water flowing through it. See *fig. 20*.

58 The remains of steps on the Inca highway. These steps zigzag up from the Vizcarra River, which was formerly crossed by the bridge of Huánuco Viejo (plate 56).

59 (*Opposite*) House foundations covering the hillside at the site of Warpo.

60 (*Opposite, below*) Typical Chupaychu house at Quero, showing remains of pitched roof, doorway and line of irregular niches across the back wall.

61 (*Above*) Excavation in progress of the altar of the Colonial church (structure III) at Ichu, showing gabled end wall of typical Chupaychu masonry. See *fig. 24*.

62 (*Below*) Doorway to structure IA at Aukimarka Alta. The state of preservation is unusually good. See *fig. 26*.

Chupaychu sites

63 Blocked niche in structure IC at Aukimarka Alta. The shape is not similar to Chupaychu niches at other sites, but rather suggests a local copy of the Inca trapezoidal niche.

64 Doorway to structure A, Aukimarka Baja, showing unusual use of corbeling. See *fig. 29*.

65 The inside of *qollqa* (storehouse) 4 at Aukimarka Alta, showing paved floor and opening on downhill side.

66 Doughnut-shaped mace or clod crusher from the surface at Ichu. The piece could have functioned either as an agricultural tool or as a weapon, or quite possibly both.

67 Effigy vessel from Aukimarka Alta, the only such vessel found during the project. The face and arms are crudely modeled on front and sides.

68 Reconstruction of part of a rim and handle of a colander from Ichu, structure I. Numerous similar but unreconstructible sherds were found in structure II, suggesting the extensive preparation of food and drink.

69 Inca Cuzco Polychrome B-style pottery from structure II, Room A at Ichu. This is the only Cuzco Polychrome pottery we found at a village site, suggesting that the occupant of the house was important.

Yacha sites

70 (*Above, left*) The tower of the Roman Catholic church in the town of Tangor. It was probably erected by Yacha masons and incorporates Yacha masonry techniques in the stone construction at the base. The town is built on top of the ancient ruins of Tangor.

71 (*Left*) View of group A at the Yacha site of Wakan, showing projecting slab steps, which ascend the wall to the intact stone roof, which may have served as a work area. See *fig. 33*.

72 (*Above*) Overview of the Yacha site of Wakan, showing how the site is built along the crest and sides of a ridge descending towards the deep river valley below.

73 (*Right*) A house at Wakan, showing overall shape and masonry technique.

Wamali sites

74 Tower at the Wamali site of Chikiarurin. This exceptionally well-preserved building has its stone roof still intact.

75 The Wamali site of Taka, showing tightly packed circular structures and towers.

76 Two-storied structure at the Wamali site of Garu. There is a stone floor between the levels. The second story would have been entered from outside.

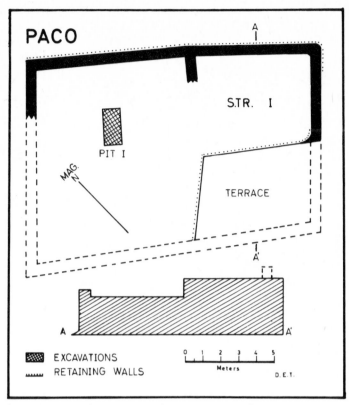

22 Plan and cross-section of structure I, a house at Paco with a terrace on one side and a courtyard in front, showing house walls which also served a retaining function.

Paco is built along the crest and sides of a low but fairly steep ridge. Clearing and limited excavation revealed houses very similar to those already described for Quero and Watuna. The major difference lay in the modification of the houses to fit the steeper and more varied terrain. The ideal square shape of the houses was often somewhat distorted in accommodating it to the irregular and narrow available spaces. In addition, many freestanding house walls also served a retaining function near their bases. Thus the rear and/or sides of a house were often partly dug into the slope. In some cases the downhill walls retained the interior floor of the houses and occasionally one common side wall was shared by two houses and by retention leveled the two floors at different heights. As the foregoing would suggest, the houses at Paco were also more densely packed on some sections of the ridge than were the houses built in the more gentle terrain at Quero and Watuna.

fig. 21

fig. 22

fig. 21

Nearby Warpo (Gualpo) appears very similar to Paco in most respects. Three of the squarish houses whose walls were exceptionally well preserved were measured and averaged 5 × 4.7 m on the interior. Central walls were again visible in some cases, and the ideal shapes were modified and floors

plate 59

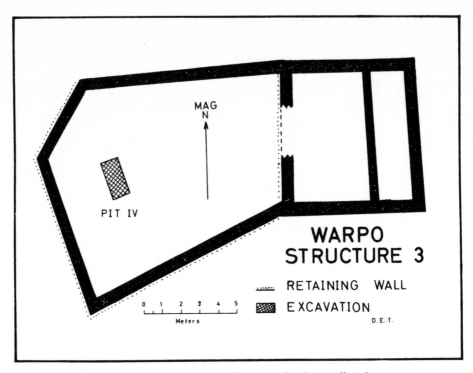

23 Plan of a house at Warpo showing a small interior dividing wall and an exterior enclosure.

fig. 23 leveled to fit the landscape. Low walls outside the doorways of some houses may have outlined adjoining enclosures or additional structures.

The *visita* of 1549 reports 19 houses for Warpo in which lived 11 Indians and 5 widows. The headman was named Paria Vilca. In 1562 the leadership had changed to Domingo Sangao, as at nearby Paco. Although we have no new house or population count, Iñigo Ortiz elsewhere reports from his visit to the village of Canchapara that in house number 4 there a couple named Miguel Llanapayco and Catalina Ruray were *mitmaq* colonists from Warpo. Their original status in Warpo is unclear, though they describe themselves as servants of the Inca emperor, Topa Inca Yupanqui. John Murra has suggested that some of these short-distance moves may have taken place after the Conquest, so their position in Canchapara is also uncertain.

Excavations at Ichu

We turn now to the most important Chupaychu site we studied, Ichu. Ichu is especially notable because it was the home of Paucar Guaman, chief of all the Chupaychu between 1542 and 1560. In the *visita* of 1549 Ichu (Ycho) is described as having 50 houses, in which dwelled 34 Indians and 12 widows. By 1562 the political importance of Ichu had declined and Ichu is only described as being under the dual headship of J. B. Guaman Chinchay and Martin Capari.

Unlike the other villages described above, where visible house remains seem to outnumber the *visita* housecounts, Ichu showed few clearly visible house remains, though those that were visible were quite spectacular. We suspect that proximity to the modern town of Panao and long use for cultivation would account for the destruction of house walls, especially those of inferior masonry. The presence of terracing and fragmentary foundation walls indicates that more houses did once exist.

Like other Chupaychu villages, Ichu lies along the crest of a ridge. Ichu's ridge, however, is close to a major tributary of the Huallaga River and is thus in much more sharply dissected terrain than that away from the principal watercourses. The ridge is therefore steep and narrow and could easily have been defended, unlike the more gentle countryside on which Quero and Watuna were built. An added attraction of Ichu's setting could also have been proximity to the products of the warm and protected ecological niche in the nearby valley bottom. Access to temperate crops, especially maize, played an important role in Inca leadership and may have been a factor in Ichu's political importance.

The remains of three principal structures are clearly visible at Ichu. Each of *fig. 24* these buildings is subdivided into two or three rooms. Each is built of rough fieldstone in mud mortar, called *pirka* masonry, but the stone was more carefully selected and fitted than in many other Chupaychu buildings. This higher quality of construction both accounts for the preservation of the buildings and suggests that the structures were important ones. The importance of the buildings is also emphasized by their location on the highest places feasible for construction on the ridge. The ridge itself was partly leveled with the aid of extensive retaining walls in order to accommodate the buildings.

Structure I, in which we did the least excavation, is built of good *pirka* masonry and was probably modified at least once after its initial construction. The present north end wall looks as though it were added later and that originally the structure was longer, a supposition supported by additional construction to the north. The north wall also partly abutted on a niche in the east wall. It is possible, however, that the building was actually constructed like structure II with end rooms, but fell in such a fashion as to suggest rebuilding. If so, structure I had no connecting doorways like those in structure II. Only with additional excavation could we hope to answer the question; and, according to our workmen, the structure has been used as a pigpen in recent times, so there may also have been several other modifications since abandonment.

The south end wall of structure I clearly had two windows in the gable. The north wall was not as clear in this respect, but appeared to have at least one window as well. Just south of center was a cross wall. Tenon stones protruded from the west side wall, presumably to help support this cross wall. There were no matching tenons in the east wall. The position of the door in this cross

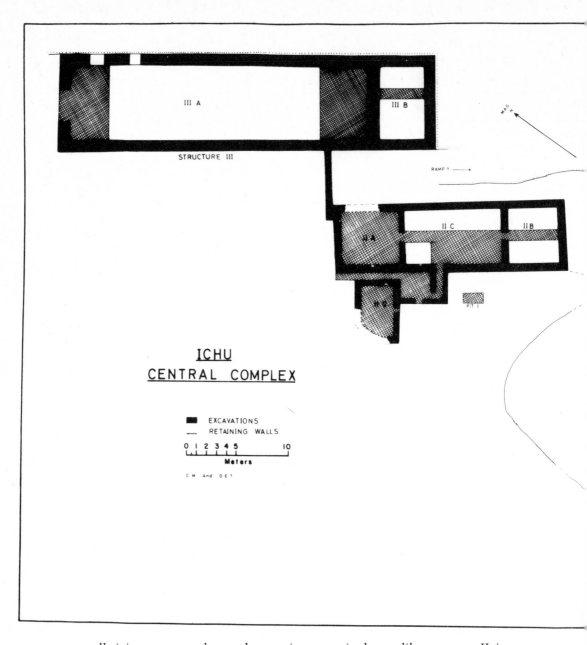

ICHU
CENTRAL COMPLEX

EXCAVATIONS
RETAINING WALLS

0 1 2 3 4 5   10
Meters

C M   And   D E T

wall giving access to the south room is uncertain, but unlike structure II, it was almost certainly not in the center. To judge by remaining cross-wall height, it was east of center. The east and south walls are retaining walls as well as freestanding ones.

One special feature of the east wall was the presence of seven niches, several of which were very regular and well made. They were the most Inca-looking niches we encountered in any Chupaychu site. As we found elsewhere, the niches had been used in modern times for offerings.

fig. 24   We paid greatest attention to structure II, which lay to the north and slightly below structure I. The main body of structure II consists of a long rectangular

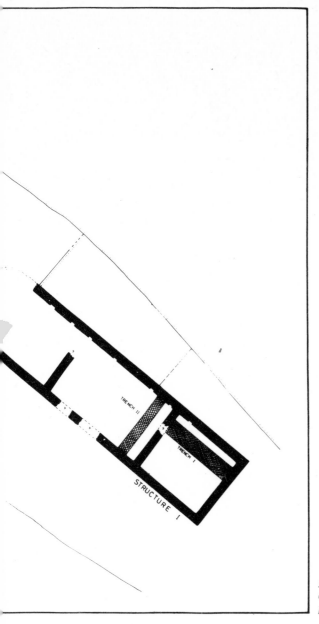

24 *Plan of the Central Complex, structures I, II, and III, at Ichu.*

building with cross walls breaking it into a square room at either end and a rectangular one between. Doorways lead from the rectangular room into the square end ones. The northwest end room was designated IIA; the southeast, IIB; and the central one, IIC. The end walls in rooms IIA and B were steeply gabled with windows in the gables and the end wall in IIA had as well a row of clearly defined squarish niches, again perhaps serving as beam sockets. The northwest wall of the same room contained two small roughly trapezoidal niches, possibly of Inca inspiration.

By comparison with the sites already described, both structures I and II are atypical for Chupaychu houses. Long and rectangular, they more closely resemble an Inca plan than a Chupaychu one. On the other hand, the cross walls divide the long rectangles into square end rooms with a rectangular one between. It is as though the Chupaychu preferred domestic form were being preserved within the confines of a long rectangle, perhaps of Inca derivation. The possible Inca influence may also be seen in the niches in the side walls of both buildings. The case is most clear in structure II; we suspect that structure I was very similar, but that remodeling in modern and perhaps much earlier times has somewhat obscured the original plan.

plates 66, 68Structure IID was in poor condition, but the room and associated passageways contained grinding stones, mortars, masses of broken pottery, ash and a probable firepit in the north corner. We are convinced that it served as a very active kitchen associated with the other rooms of structure II.

plate 69Pottery will be discussed in more detail later, but it would be appropriate to mention here that structures I and II contained both typical Chupaychu pottery like that found in other villages and Inca inspired wares, probably made by local potters. In addition, room IIA contained several pieces of Inca-style Cuzco Polychrome B, or a good local copy thereof. Inca-inspired shapes do occur in other Chupaychu villages, perhaps as a result of local potters having to make pottery to Inca specifications for tribute purposes, for pottery is a recorded item of tribute in the *visitas*. However, Inca polychrome pottery has never been found by us in other village sites.

The presence of Cuzco Polychrome here at Ichu, together with the high quality of the masonry in structures I and II and the unusual, perhaps Inca-inspired, rectangular plans and trapezoidal niches, have convinced us that these structures housed the chief of the Chupaychus, Paucar Guaman, himself, together perhaps with some of his relatives. Since it was Inca policy to rule through the local leadership, these Inca traits and the obvious importance of the buildings would be reflections of the status of the occupants in the Inca political system. The separate, heavily used, kitchen is also indicative of high status, because under the Andean systems of reciprocity it was the obligation of the leaders to provide abundant food and drink to those who served under them.

Structure III is quite different. Much longer than structures I and II or any known Chupaychu building, it had in addition a very wide door at one end and a narrow rectangular room (IIIB) at the other. The masonry, however, is typical of Chupaychu construction, and the wall opposite the doorway, between the long room and the small one, shows the remains of a gable and possibly a window as in structure II. Virtually no pottery was found in the fill of the main long room (IIIA), but a good deal came from the small room, IIIB, suggesting, with the size difference, separate functions for the two rooms.

plate 61Excavation across the end of the long room (IIIA) opposite the wide door revealed a masonry block built against the center of the wall. It was set on a low platform built across the end of the room and the platform was ascended by three steps. There is no doubt in our minds that we have here the remains of the Colonial-period Roman Catholic church, with perhaps a storeroom, sacristy, or residence attached to the rear.

We do not know the exact dates for the church yet, but it is unlikely that it was built before 1540, and is probably later. It was most likely abandoned, along with Ichu itself, in the 1570s under the *reducción* policy of Viceroy Francisco de Toledo, a plan which brought Indians down from their remote villages to common, Spanish-designed centers for political control and religious indoctrination. A bell in the belfry of the church in the nearby town of Panao is said to have come from Ichu, but we were unable to ascertain the bell's date, which was not visible on the casting. Ichu is believed by some of the local people to be the dwelling place of a supernatural bell which tolls on certain days in the religious calendar. This is a widespread Andean belief, but in the case of Ichu, a real bell may have rung in the Colonial period and the memory may persist in this folk belief.

At Ichu, then, we no doubt have a continuous occupation from an undetermined pre-Inca date, through the period of Inca domination, to sometime in the 1570s under Spanish Colonial rule. The village, moreover, was an important one in Inca and Colonial times, a fact that is reflected not only in the *visitas*, but also in the archaeological remains of artifacts, ceramics, and impressive atypical architecture.

The enigmatic site of Aukimarka

The last Chupaychu village to be considered, Aukimarka, is located upstream from the modern city of Huánuco on the right side of the Huallaga River. If one follows the river valley, Aukimarka is a long way from Ichu and the other Pachitea Andina villages, for the river does a great rightangle bend just below Huánuco. It is much closer to Pachitea Andina over the intervening high country, the hypotenuse, so to speak. The local Indians follow the shorter high-country routes today and undoubtedly did so in the past as well.

Aukimarka is built along the crest of a high ridge overlooking the Huallaga River, a location similar to that of Ichu and some of the other Chupaychu villages. At Aukimarka more extensive use was made of terracing to produce large flat areas for habitation than was the case in the other Chupaychu sites. The site seems to break down into upper and lower zones, which we have called Aukimarka Alta (upper) and Aukimarka Baja (lower). Not only is there a clear separation of the site into these upper and lower zones, but also the architecture is distinctive in each of the two sections. The buildings appear in addition to be much more densely packed together in the lower part. We are undecided if this division is in any way related to the Inca social divisions, *hanansaya* (upper) and *urinsaya* (lower), since these moieties are rare in the Huánuco area except in places established by the Inca themselves. In Huánuco the dual function is taken over by the *allauca* (right) and *ichoc* (left) divisions, as was brought out in our discussion of Inca bridges in Chapter 7.

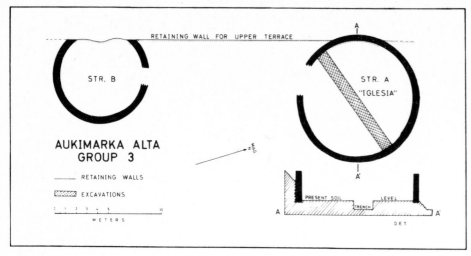

The most striking of the two zones is Aukimarka Alta, for it contains impressive buildings which are totally different from those in the other Chupaychu villages discussed above. Most of them are also very different from *fig. 25* Inca structures. Rectangular buildings are present, but most distinctive is a group of at least eight large circular houses, six of them built in pairs with their single doorways facing one another across flat open spaces. Nowhere else in Chupaychu territory did we find such buildings; we found the nearest comparable structures in Wamali sites in the drainage of the Upper Marañón River. These are discussed in Chapter 9.

fig. 26 The circular houses are large, up to 10.5 m in diameter. In some cases *plate 62* sections of wall still stand up to their original height. In house IA a complete doorway was preserved with both its sill and lintel in place. Two drilled stones, which presumably were related to the functioning of the door itself, projected into the room on either side of the doorway. At least five stones project from the wall in the interior of house IA, and two small windows pierce the wall. Floors were not found in excavation, but we suspect that since they were not protected by fallen wall debris, they have probably been destroyed by cultivation and perhaps by use of the buildings as pens. We assume the roofs were conical, but excavation revealed no evidence of central post supports.

There were also the foundations of a series of rectangular rooms at Aukimarka Alta. One of these, structure IC, seems to be associated with the two facing circular structures, IA and B. It was badly fallen, but in its walls *plate 63* were preserved two niches, one of which had been clearly blocked up in recent times, because a bottle, probably an offering again, was visible behind the stones. These niches do not resemble the irregular Chupaychu ones found in Pachitea Andina, but neither do they look purely Inca. We suspect that they could be provincial Inca, local if somewhat unsuccessful attempts to copy the Inca style.

Other rectangular buildings, such as those in group 2, are difficult to *figs. 27, 28* classify. Walls were not preserved to a sufficient height to observe whether or not masonry gables were present. Low walls such as these could, of course,

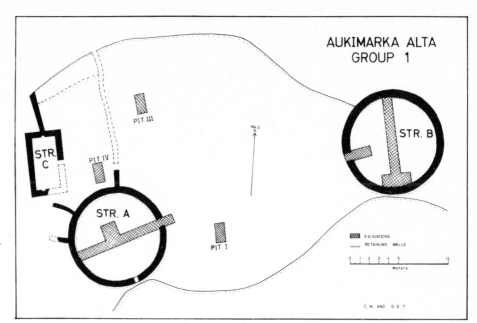

26 Group 1 at Aukimarka Alta, consisting of a pair of circular structures facing one another on a terrace and an associated small rectangular building. See plate 62.

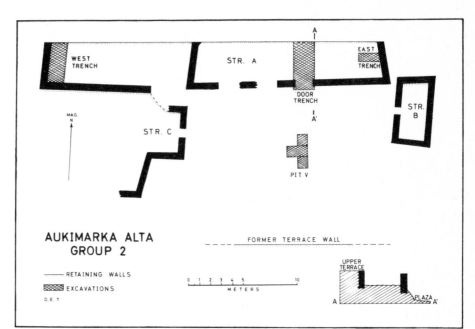

27 Group 2 at Aukimarka Alta, consisting of rectangular buildings built on a terrace with the rear walls serving a retaining function in part.

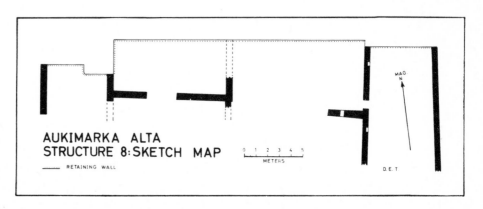

28 A sketch map of structure 8 at Aukimarka Alta, consisting of a series of straight walls outlining what was probably a group of rectangular structures similar to Group 2 (fig. 27). The rear walls also serve a retaining function.

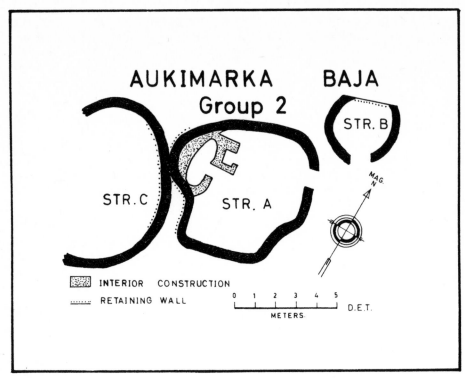

29 Group 2 at Aukimarka Baja, illustrating the irregular shapes of houses. Structures A and B are directly associated; structure C faces away at a lower level. See plate 64.

have served as foundations for adobe walls, which had since eroded away. The proportions of the rooms, like those of the niches, again looked neither Chupaychu nor purely Inca.

Aukimarka Baja presents a very different impression. The structures are much more densely packed together, and the wall preservation is not as good. The quality of the masonry appears to be inferior, which would account for the greater state of ruin in Aukimarka Baja, but another contributing factor could well have been greater use of the area for cultivation after the abandonment of the village. The combination of poor wall preservation, densely packed construction and heavy plant cover make it difficult to discern building types and arrangements, but it appears that the pairs of large circular buildings characteristic of Aukimarka Alta are absent and that the structures which are present are smaller and very inconsistently shaped, varying from rectangular to roughly circular to oval to U-shaped to highly irregular. We also have the impression from the standing wall heights that greater use may have been made of perishable materials in the construction.

fig. 29 The complexities of Aukimarka Baja are well illustrated by group 2, which contained better-preserved buildings than usual in that zone, and was examined and recorded as an example of the architecture of Aukimarka Baja.

Structure A was very irregular in plan and had some low interior construction of unknown function to the rear, opposite the door. It looks as though the interior construction outlined an oval chamber that had originally been roofed by slabs. The doorway of structure A was quite differently shaped from those preserved in Aukimarka Alta. The two sides of the doorway curved markedly inward near the top of corbeling. Presumably the false arch was completed by a capstone or lintel, which has since disappeared. The use of the corbeled arch and vault is not known from other Chupaychu sites in Pachitea Andina, though it does occur in the drainage of the Upper Marañón in Wamali sites and in *mitmaq* sites on the left side on the Huallaga River.

plate 64

Structure B was roughly circular. The side opposite the door, however, was straight where it had been built into the slope and thus was also performing a retaining function. The doorway itself opened into the same space at rightangles and close to that of structure A. Structure C was oval to c-shaped in plan, and clearly did not share the same frontal space as the other two buildings. It was probably part of another group, since its doorway faced the opposite direction from structure A and opened onto a lower level. Other buildings at Aukimarka Baja showed similar variation in size plan, and orientation.

One outstanding feature at Aukimarka Baja was the presence of a row of four well-built, small and fairly well-preserved circular structures. We are virtually certain these functioned as storehouses or *qollqa* built under Inca influence. All of them had small low openings on the downhill side and high ones on the uphill side. The floors of three of them were paved with stone slabs. The system of roofing is uncertain, but the openings mentioned above are so small that access to the contents of the storehouses must have been from

fig. 30
plate 65

30 The storehouses or 'qollqa' at Aukimarka. See plate 65.

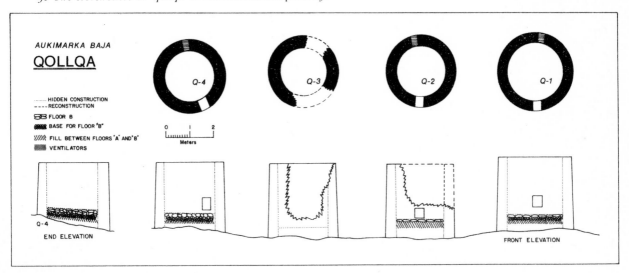

147

the top. Such rooftop access seems to have been the case in many Inca *qollqa* at Huánuco Pampa as well.[62]

We found no other structures like these storehouses at the village level except at one other site, Garu, which will be discussed with the Wamali sites in Chapter 9. Yet they resemble Imperial Inca warehouses in location, arrangement in a row, and overall design. The main difference from Inca examples is size; the Aukimarka *qollqa* are smaller than most Inca ones. We are uncertain how to explain their presence at Aukimarka. Were they a deliberate local copy of imperial storage for local prestige by emulation? Were they a local storage facility which was locally operated as part of the Imperial Inca system, a waystation or local collection point, for example? Or were they Inca owned, built and operated? We feel the last alternative is the least likely since they look locally constructed, are so few in number, and the Inca tended to rule through the existing structures. Their presence along with some other evidence, however, does serve to indicate a strong Inca influence here at the local level despite the non-Inca look of much of the rest of the architecture.

Chupaychu pottery

The ceramics associated with Chupaychu sites offer some interesting but limited additional information. Unfortunately, we were able to detect little stratigraphic evidence for cultural changes through time, probably because the sites are located on steep ridges which impeded neat horizontal deposition, but perhaps also because the occupation was not long enough to allow deep accumulations of midden. What is clear, however, is that the ceramic collections represent a local tradition of pottery making blended with influence from the conquering Incas.

In Pachitea Andina there was remarkable ceramic consistency among the sites. For those familiar with the highly polished and painted or intricately modeled ceramics of the Peruvian coast, the pottery of these remote villages will appear rather plain and sometimes quite crude. It is almost entirely oxidized-fired redware, showing at best remnants of a red slip. Most of it is quite crude, thick and not fired very hard.

One of the most distinctive features of Pachitea Andina Chupaychu pottery is the use of clay containing a lot of rather large pieces of mica and resulting in a glittering surface, which looks as though it were covered with small sequins. We have named this pottery 'micaceous ware.' We do not yet know whether the mica was deliberately added to the clay as a temper or if it was simply present in one of the clay sources used by Chupaychu potters. Although this micaceous pasta is very distinctive, it makes up only about ten percent of the collections.

The distribution of the micaceous pottery is also very important. It is absent at Aukimarka. Aukimarka is recorded in the *visita* of Iñigo Ortiz as a Chupaychu village, but, as was brought out above, it has architecture unlike that found at Pachitea Andina. Ceramic differences appear to parallel the architectural ones, as will be discussed in greater detail below. On the other hand, a few pieces of typical Chupaychu micaceous pottery have been found at Huánuco Pampa. This would seem to indicate either the presence of Chupaychu residents at Huánuco Pampa or the shipment of Chupaychu-made pottery as tribute to the site. Both explanations are consistent with known Inca policy, for pottery is recorded as an item of tribute in the documents, and it is very likely that Chupaychus served at Huánuco Pampa as part of their *mit'a* service to the state.

Almost all the remaining Pachitea Andina Chupaychu pottery can be classified as plainware or red-slipped ware, though in some examples of the latter, the red slip is very fugitive, implying that a number of seemingly plain sherds may originally have been slipped. The slip itself varies from an orangish red, which is sloppily applied, to a deep red, which is evenly applied and closely resembles Inca redwares. It would be tempting to conclude that the former is in the local tradition and the latter, Inca derived, but there is only a little stratigraphic evidence to support this view, and it is equally likely that the poorly slipped orangish pottery is a local adaptation of Inca slipping. We strongly suspect that the Inca demanded that pottery for their use be made to their specifications and that local potters, in meeting this demand, adopted some of the Inca ideas for local use as well.

The same kind of problem arises in the study of shapes. There are clear examples of Inca flaring rims, complete with pierced nodes, but there are also flaring rims that are shaped and thickened in a fashion not found in true Cuzco Inca pottery. Again, this may well represent a local adaptation of an Inca idea.

It is in handle construction that the local tradition most clearly asserts itself. The Inca made extensive use of thin, parallel-sided strap handles, and these handles do occasionally turn up in Pachitea Andina Chupaychu sites. Far more common, however, are thick, finger-indented, pulled handles, which appear to be in the purely local tradition. The attachment is also distinctive; local handles are surrounded with much more clay filler, producing very thick bases to the handles.

Returning to Aukimarka, we observe not only the absence of the micaceous pottery, but also the presence of a surface treatment that is not found in Pachitea Andina sites. We have named this 'black crackled ware.' It is rare but distinctive in the Aukimarka collections and also occurs rarely at Yacha sites. As the name implies, the exterior surface has a crackled appearance, usually black but sometimes reddish. It appears as though the makers added a slip which shrank more than the pottery surface to which it was applied, thus producing the crackling. We suspect that the original slip was red and that it became blackened in firing or in the subsequent use of the vessel in cooking fires. Aukimarka also appears to have some slightly different rim forms and handle shapes. In addition, the site yielded our only example of a human effigy   plate 67
vessel.

Summary

To sum up, all our archaeological data from Pachitea Andina Chupaychu sites is in keeping with the view of a local ethnic group with internal consistency coming under the control of the Inca empire. Under Inca rule they adopted some aspects of Inca culture, especially those in keeping with the new political order, such as the elaborate houses and Imperial Inca pottery in the Chupaychu chief's village of Ichu. In addition, some aspects of Inca pottery making filtered down to the local level and merged with the Chupaychu tradition, probably at the instigation of the local potters, who made pottery to Inca specifications for Inca use. For reasons of novelty, prestige, practicality or habit, some of these Inca traits were adopted for local use. This ceramic situation is in contrast to the architecture, which remained purely local in design with the one exception of Ichu, where the local chief represented the Inca, and his more Inca-looking and elaborate house reflects his status in the imperial political system.

Aukimarka, by contrast, is different in both ceramics and architecture from the Pachitea Andina Chupaychu sites. As John Murra has pointed out, these differences add weight to the suggestion in the *visita* that Aukimarka was added to the Chupaychu ethnic unit in post-Conquest times, probably for the convenience of the Spaniards. Here then we have another good case for the archaeological data clarifying and enlarging upon the ethnohistoric record. We know far more about what went on in Huánuco from immediately pre-Inca to Colonial times from a combination of the written record and the archaeology than we could from either source alone.

Many problems remain, however. For example, the ethnohistoric record sheds no light on Aukimarka's unusual circular houses, which are unlike both the other Chupaychu and the neighboring Yacha ones. They most closely resemble Wamali houses from the Upper Marañón. It is possible that some Wamali *mitmaq* colonists were moved to Aukimarka by the Inca or perhaps even by the Spaniards in the early Colonial period. So far, however, we have no other lines of evidence to support such a suggestion.

9 Ethnic diversity in the Huánuco region

During the course of our survey in the Huánuco area we studied two other ethnic groups, though we devoted much less time to them than to the Chupaychu. These two groups, the Yacha and the Wamali, provide a sharp contrast both to each other and to the Chupaychu. Our discussion of them will be less detailed but will emphasize the high degree of ethnic diversity that existed in the area prior to the imposition of Inca rule. We suspect that much of this diversity persisted under the Incas and well into the Spanish Colonial period. Indeed, remnants of these ancient affiliations may even be observed today.[63]

For one of these groups, the Yacha, we have documentation in the *visita* of Iñigo Ortiz; the other group, the Wamali, was not included in the *visita*, but its proximity to Huánuco Pampa makes it virtually certain that its members also served that center and were probably active in the building and maintenance of the road north of Huánuco Pampa and the *tampu* of Taparaku. Most of the Yacha, like the Chupaychu, are located on the Huallaga River drainage; the Wamali and a few of the Yacha, by contrast, are near the headwaters of the Marañón River. The major Inca installations of Huánuco Pampa itself, the *tampu* of Tunsucancha and Taparaku, and the associated highway running between them are also located nearby in the Marañón drainage. To judge by the evidence in the Espinoza Campos document on Inca bridges discussed in Chapter 7, the closest local villagers were responsible for the maintenance of bridges and perhaps the associated road. Moreover, the *visita* of Iñigo Ortiz specifically states that the Yachas served at the *tampu* of Tunsucancha. We therefore feel it is virtually certain that both the Wamali and the Yacha were very active in the construction and maintenance of the Inca installations which were located immediately adjacent to their respective homelands.

The Yacha of the upper Marañón

Our first survey in Yacha territory took us on a brief visit to the area around Cauri (Caure), a northern extension of the Yacha domain on the drainage of the upper Marañón, very close to what we believe to be the boundary with the Wamali. There we briefly surveyed two archaeological sites near the modern town of Cauri: Cauricancha, which is almost certainly the site of the old Cauri,

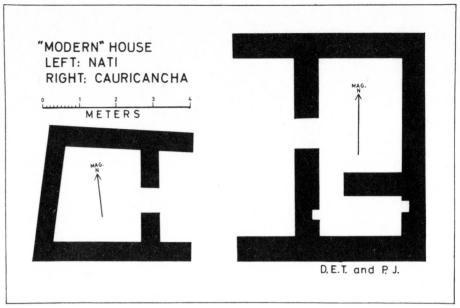

"MODERN" HOUSE
LEFT: NATI
RIGHT: CAURICANCHA

METERS

MAG. N

MAG. N

D. E. T. and P. J.

31 Plan of a ruined rectangular house at Cauricancha and one at Nati. These are almost certainly post-Conquest, but conservative in their architecture, the projecting side walls being a fairly rare feature today except in churches or in houses in quite remote areas.

and Nati (Nate, Natín), both of which were included in the 1562 visit of Iñigo Ortiz. They lie to the southeast on a river terrace 200–300 m above the modern town.

Cauricancha occupies a small flat pampa and the gentle slopes above it. The site is unfortunately very badly disturbed from the construction of modern houses, which are currently being lived in, and many corrals for the residents' animals. The area is high, close to the upper limits of cultivation, and herding is very important today. There are numerous remains of small terraced fields at the site. These are the kind of terraces that are the result of the cultivation and some modification of the slope rather than the elaborate planned stone-walled terrace systems found in Inca sites to the south near Cuzco. Despite the destruction, the foundations of circular and rectangular houses are visible. We counted thirty-one circular houses and were able to measure twenty-one of them, which ranged in interior diameter between 4.7 m and 6.65 m, averaging 5.84 m. Where the wall height permitted, we were able to observe single doorways in the walls. Two houses also had the remains of an interior wall which made an arc from one side of the doorway to a point just short of the opposite side, thus dividing off a lens-shaped interior room amounting to between a quarter and a third of the total interior space.

fig. 31   The rectangular houses are probably Colonial period or later in date. They make use of a design by which the side walls project a short distance in front of the building, producing a small walled porch area. This is a conservative form

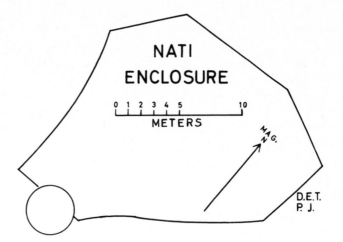

NATI
ENCLOSURE

0 1 2 3 4 5   10
METERS

MAG. N.

D.E.T.
P. J.

32 Plan of a circular house and its associated enclosure at Nati. The walls were too badly fallen to note the position of the door to the circular house.

of architecture found today in the older houses and in remote villages of the area. The plan is also seen in local village church architecture, which tends to be very conservative. There is also an open space resembling a plaza at the site, at one end of which lies a fairly large rectangular building measuring 4.55 × 11.35 m. But the date of the building and the plaza remain uncertain.

Nati, which is only a little over five minutes walk from Cauricancha, was combined with Cauri in the *visita*. Like Cauricancha, it is badly disturbed by modern construction, farming, and grazing, and an accurate original house count would likewise be impossible without excavation. We measured seven houses, which ranged in diameter from a dubious small one of 3.2 m to 6.9 m, with an average of 5.2 m. There are also enclosure walls, perhaps corrals, of unknown date and some irregular terraces like those described for Cauricancha.

fig. 32

In his *visita*, Iñigo Ortiz combined these two communities in his summary figures. In both cases the headman was named Pablo Almerco and the *cacique*, Antonio Guaynacapcha. Ortiz recorded 35 houses in Cauri and 6 in Nati, counting a total of 168 people. These break down into 34 married couples, 3 couples living together, 1 widow, 10 bachelors, 9 single women, 10 boys and 11 girls aged 7 to 12, 11 boys and 15 girls aged 3 to 7, 12 boys and 7 girls aged 3 or under, 1 old man who still worked, 2 old women who still worked, and 5 old women who no longer worked. There is some discrepancy between the figures quoted by the headman, Almerco, the individual house counts, and the summary figures. Since there are problems over the interpretation of how some people are counted, we have quoted the summary figures.

The combination of the archaeology, ethnohistory and ethnology of Cauri and Nati present some interesting problems. The area is high, good for high-altitude crops and herding, a zone called *jalga* in Quechua. Herding is important today and probably was also in the past to judge by the corrals, some of which are almost certainly ancient. Yet in 1562 at the time of the *visita*, although the local people admitted that they had many pastures, only 59 camelids, 29 pigs and 13 European sheep were recorded in general testimony. Fewer yet were recorded in the individual house counts. One wonders if animals were being hidden or if many were at their higher pastures and not counted, either out of error on the part of Iñigo Ortiz or design on the part of the informants. Modern Cauri is virtually deserted today during that part of the year when the animals are being kept in their higher pastures. Perhaps it was when Iñigo Ortiz passed through.

The people of Cauri apparently had access to fields at lower altitude, the zone called *kechwa*, where more temperate crops such as maize could be grown. As Cezar Fonseca has described in detail, these lands, which lay in the Yacha territory of Chaupiwaranga, were lost in post-Conquest times, but the economic relationship persists even today. Formal trade relationships exist by which high-altitude products are exchanged for temperate ones in the areas of former ownership. Thus, though the mechanism has changed, the relationship and access persist.[64]

As noted earlier, the Yacha at Cauri and Nati form a northern extension of Yacha territory. Just downstream from Cauri lies the boundary with the Wamali. Fonseca again makes the interesting ethnographic observation that the residents of modern Cauri have much closer social relationships with the former Yacha territory of Chaupiwaranga far to the south than they do with their much closer neighbors just downstream in Jesus, a town we believe to be within the former Wamali territory and perhaps even a Wamali *reducción*.

From an architectural point of view the houses at Cauri and Nati are circular and do not resemble the Yacha houses at lower altitude in Chaupiwaranga to be described below. They are somewhat more comparable to Wamali houses from downstream on the Marañón, though they are considerably smaller in size. They most closely resemble some of the houses in a very high-altitude site belonging to a group called the Quero, who are believed to be former Yachas reorganized by the Inca. This site, called Wamalli and not to be confused with the ethnic group of similar name, has been described by Ramiro Matos and will be briefly discussed below.

Finally, the *visita* indicates that the Inca moved pottery makers from Cauri to Tangor, a town in Chaupiwaranga to be described next. This would suggest that pottery making was once a local industry in Cauri. According to Cézar Fonseca, pottery is not made in Cauri today, nor has it been within the memory of the local inhabitants. A detailed archaeological study might show similarities in the ceramics of the two areas, but our sample was too small to verify this. Even extensive excavation would probably not reveal kilns, since firing was probably done in the open.

The Yacha and the Huallaga drainage

Tangor (Tancor) which, as noted above, lies in Chaupiwaranga in the Huallaga drainage and had pottery makers brought from Cauri, lies underneath the

Colonial and modern town of the same name. At the edges and in open sections of the town, one can still see the remains of ancient walls and a light scatter of broken pottery. Most of the ancient Tangor probably lies under the buildings and plaza of the modern town, and the destruction of what remains is too great to allow plans to be drawn. We suspect that old Tangor was dismantled to build modern Tangor, which was probably a *reducción* of several Yacha communities from the immediate area. Even the present-day architecture has a very conservative and local ethnic look about it, suggesting that native masons made the buildings to Spanish specifications but incorporated details from their own architectural tradition as well.

plate 70

It is impossible to discuss the architecture or size of Tangor in any detail because of the destruction of the older buildings, but we have the impression that it was much bigger than the house count of three houses in the *visita* would indicate. This discrepancy can be explained by the indication in the *visita* that only the houses of persons included in the *encomienda* of Juan Sanchez Falcon were counted; those belonging to two other *encomiendas* appear to have been omitted. The reasons for this situation have been discussed by Enrique Meyer in some detail and need not concern us here. Of greater concern is the distinct possibility that other towns may have inaccurate house counts for similar reasons; or, as Meyer also suggests, because it was to the advantage of the local people to reduce the population figures in order to lessen their tribute payments. In short, they may have resisted giving the information requested in the *visita* in 1562, just as they resist similar governmental census-taking today, as Meyer has described it in 1971.[65]

Wakan, an archaeological site about 4 km away, provides a very sharp contrast to Tangor. It is built along the crest and sides of a ridge which descends sharply toward the river valley far below. It is in an excellent state of preservation and thus allows a detailed examination of Chaupiwaranga Yacha architecture.[66]

fig. 72

The buildings at Wakan are quite different from those at Chupaychu sites, at the other Yacha sites of Cauri and Nati, and at Wamali sites to be discussed shortly. The structures tend to be rectangular to oval in plan, with rounded interior corners, which produce a generally oval interior shape. There is a lot of variation in the shapes of buildings, in part an accommodation no doubt to the steep terrain and narrow confines of the ridge. The walls of many buildings, as is the case in other ridge-crest villages, serve a retaining function to level the slope as well as to form the wall of the room. So steep is the slope, indeed, that in some places access to a house may be over the roof of a lower one. The oval interiors tend to be small, with the walls containing projecting stones and usually niches in the corners. Today these niches often contain human skulls and long bones, though the date of their placement is uncertain. Small bones are absent, and, as is frequently the case elsewhere, there are indications of modern religious use of the structures.

figs. 33–35

The roofs are usually flat and made of slabs of stone set across the partially

plates 71, 73

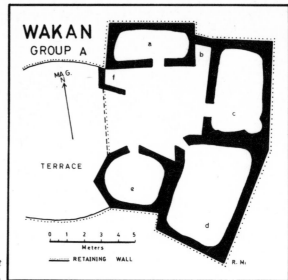

33 *House group A at Wakan. See plate 71.*

corbeled walls. The exteriors of the buildings sometimes have sets of ascending projecting stones, which appear to have served as steps to ascend to the roof. We suspect that the flat roofs were used as work areas or for drying food. Space would have been at a premium in such a tightly packed village. The solution of using roof space is unusual in the Andean area, though it is found elsewhere in the world – in the pueblos of the American Southwest, for example.

Ramiro Matos, in his more detailed study of this village, estimated its overall size at about 100 × 200 m and concluded that there were sixty-six living units and one central public building, probably of religious function. The houses were usually grouped around a small courtyard, which was sometimes

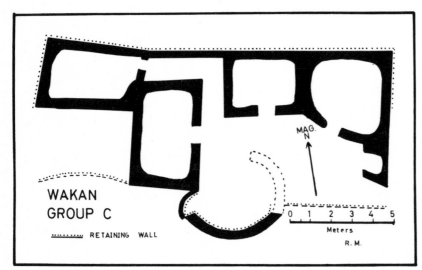

34 *House group C at Wakan.*

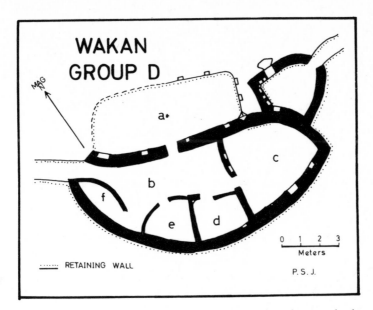

35 House group D
at Wakan.

paved and sometimes contained stone-lined subterranean chambers, which presumably served for storage. We did not encounter such underground chambers elsewhere in Huánuco, though they do occur inside houses in villages lower down in the Marañón drainage. As noted earlier, storage could well have taken place in attics under the pitched roofs of Chupaychu houses.

The central communal building has two side towers, each about 7 m high with a two-story building between them. The structure is riddled with a dozen small chambers and seems to have served as a charnel house, perhaps among other functions. The building is similar to ones found in the upper Marañón drainage.

Interestingly, though Tangor lies nearby and Iñigo Ortiz must have passed very close to Wakan on his journey of inspection, no mention of Wakan is made by any of the informants in the *visita*. This raises the interesting question of why it was omitted. Small amounts of Inca pottery at the site suggest that an occupation did survive into the period of Inca domination. One might speculate that the inhabitants were moved away by the Inca, as clearly happened elsewhere according to the Spanish records, or that the village was abandoned early in the Colonial period for unknown reasons. Alternatively, perhaps it was still occupied at the time of the *visita* but was omitted by Iñigo Ortiz either because its existence was hidden from him, which seems unlikely, or because the inhabitants, like some of those at Tangor, belonged to an *encomienda* not included in the *visita*. We are inclined to favor the last explanation, since a longer occupation would at least partly account for the remarkable state of preservation of some of the buildings.

In commenting on another Yacha village in Chaupiwaranga called Wapia (Guapia), which was visited by Iñigo Ortiz, Matos notes that the masonry, *fig. 36* while certainly in the local Yacha tradition, was rather careless in its

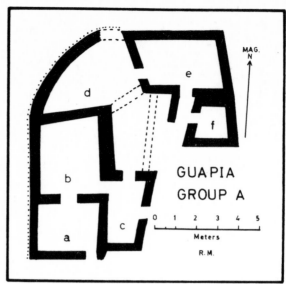

*36 House group
A at Guapia*

construction but that the evidence for Inca influence was also stronger than at Wakan. We did not visit this site and it has not yet been published, so we will refrain from further comment except to note this slight contrast to Wakan.

We did not study the ethnic group called the Queros in the *visita* in any detail during the project. As noted in Chapter 3, the Queros were apparently originally considered as Yachas, but were separated from them by the Inca, Huayna Capac. Matos did visit and describe one site called Wamalli in the Queros territory. Unfortunately, it was not one of the villages visited by Iñigo Ortiz so we have no ethnohistoric data on it except that it is within what we believe to be the pre-Inca Yacha ethnic unit on the basis of testimony and the proximity of the site to others which were included in the *visita*.

Matos describes the site of Wamalli as being located in high-altitude grassland or *puna* at approximately 3,800 m. It covers an area of about 4 hectares and contains some 120 dwellings. It is clearly divided into three sections. The upper part contains forty-six *qollqa* or storehouses, a relatively rare feature indicating Inca affiliation and recalling the Chupaychu site of Aukimarka discussed in Chapter 8 and the Wamali site of Garu to be discussed below. The central section appears to be residential. It was made up of forty-eight rectangular structures composed of two to six rooms which communicated with one another by means of trapezoidal doorways. Streets and passageways ran between the houses and there was a central plaza and a water cistern. This arrangement is also suggestive of some Inca influence. The lowest section was the largest and most spread out. It consisted of roughly circular houses incorporated into large corrals with their doorways oriented inward.

The only evidence for a communal building at the site was a small circular structure built well above the village by a rockshelter. The building was approached by a path with stone steps, and within it were two small burial chambers.

Wamalli, then, appears to have an Inca component in its storage area and perhaps in its central residential section. The lower zone, with its corrals and circular structures, most clearly resembles the Yacha sites of Cauri and Nati, which are also at high altitude and were apparently oriented toward herding activities. When we compare these sites with those in Chaupiwaranga, it seems as though there is an internal ethnic differentiation of architecture associated with altitude and/or economic base. The sample is too small and the affiliations too confused to be sure, but it is an impression worth further investigation.

The Wamali

The Wamali, not to be confused with the site of similar name discussed above, make up the third ethnic group we investigated. Because the Wamali were not included in the *visita* of Iñigo Ortiz, we spent much less time on them than on the other groups and on the Inca, but we carried out enough limited survey to provide a basis for comparison with the Yacha and the Chupaychu. Although we are neither sure of the boundaries of the Wamali nor certain of the ethnic affiliation of all the sites, nonetheless our results do emphasize once again the high degree of ethnic diversity to be found in the Huánuco area.[67]

One of the best examples of what we believe to be a Wamali site is called Garu. Garu is built along the crest and adjacent sides of a ridge high above the Marañón Valley. The masonry is of well-fitted and chinked rough stone with a high proportion of flat slab. Especially striking are the ruins of very large oval to circular houses. One such structure measured 9.8 × 8.25 m on the interior and had its walls still standing to a height of 2.2 m. The doorway had a high sill and was trapezoidal in shape, measuring 88 cm across the top, 92 cm across the bottom and 1.5 m high. These large round houses sometimes appear to have been built in pairs facing one another across small flattened spaces resembling plazas. They immediately remind one of the Chupaychu site of Aukimarka discussed in Chapter 8. Unlike Aukimarka, however, Garu also has a two-storied structure with a stone floor between the stories, the remains of a multi-storied tower, and a corbeled vaulted tomb. These are all typical of the architecture of Wamali sites but are not found at Aukimarka.

Below the ridge crest proper but high on the slope was a row of ten circular structures which were undoubtedly *qollqa*. All had small openings on the downhill side and some at least had high windows on the uphill side. The masonry was slightly different from that found above at Garu proper; a higher proportion of round stones had been used, accompanied by more mud mortar, in contrast to the greater use of slab above. The spaces between the *qollqa* were filled, making a wall of the row, and this *qollqa* wall formed the downhill side of a rectangular enclosure or corral built above the storehouses. The one *qollqa* measured had an interior diameter of 3.35 m. We have already raised

plate IX

plate 76

plate X

the problem of the function of Inca storehouses at village sites in our discussion of the *qollqa* at the Chupaychu site of Aukimarka in Chapter 8. The same arguments would apply here except that the problem is compounded by Garu's being so close to Huánuco Pampa that local state storage would seem unnecessary. There is also a lower section of Garu which is currently being lived in and which we did not investigate.

plate 75   Other Wamali sites are generally similar, though they vary in detail. Taka, across the Marañón river valley from Garu, shares a similar location on a ridge and a settlement pattern of tightly packed structures. There are circular to D-shaped houses, rectangular buildings, and towers which are roughly rectangular in plan but have one or more bowed walls. Diagonal lines of exterior projecting stones sometimes occur and permit one to ascend to the roofs. The roofs, which are still intact in some cases, are of big stone slabs set over partly corbeled interior walls.

Earlier in the chapter in our discussion of the Yacha sites of Nati and Cauricancha we mentioned that we believed that they were close to the border with the Wamali. Just a few kilometers downstream from Cauri there are several sites, including two we visited called Markachakra and Alaka, which are very similar to Garu and Taka in their ridge-crest location and in the presence of large circular structures, towers and other less well-defined plate 74 buildings. There is also one site called Chikiarurin which has similar structures, including some very well-preserved towers, but which, unlike the other Wamali sites, is located on the flat valley bottom. We are inclined to believe that Chikiarurin is a *reducción*, possibly of Inca date, but more likely of the Colonial period. This supposition is partly supported by the presence of a large rectangular building which once had a gabled roof and which looks more like a church than anything the Wamali ever built.

From these brief comments it should be clear that the Wamali are quite unlike the Inca, and are also unlike the neighboring Yacha and Chupaychu. Huánuco was characterized by ethnic diversity. The presence of locally made Inca ceramic traits, however, indicates that the Wamali were incorporated into the empire, and, although we so far lack the Colonial-period documentation, we can safely assume that, like the Yacha and Chupaychu, they paid labor service and worked at nearby state installations. We are also sure that like the others, they were administered through the pre-existing local political structure, though we are not yet in a position to name the town of the chief and to excavate his house as we were in the case of the Chupaychu.

The *mitmaq* colonists

Before ending our discussion of local ethnic groups, we should say a few words about the *mitmaq* villages (colonists from outside the area). The *visitas* make it clear that there were such villages in Huánuco, but we had little time to find or investigate them during the initial project. The problem of studying such villages is made especially difficult by the fact that there existed both completely *mitmaq* towns and towns with local residents plus *mitmaq* families from one or more places of origin.

One of the potentially most interesting *mitmaq* areas was a small tributary valley of the Huallaga which contained two communities called Llanquipampa and Malconga. The *visita* of 1549 records that these communities had *mitmaq* families from Chachapoyas, far to the north, and 'Cayanbes,' presumably from Ecuador. Although we made several trips to the area, our survey results were very disappointing. We located a number of very badly destroyed walls that were probably once part of a village and picked up a collection of rather eroded and non-descript pottery. There appears to be some potentially interesting material for study there, but intensive survey and excavation would be major undertakings and logistically quite difficult.

We also located and visited the *mitmaq* site of Warapa (Huarapa, Guarapa). The village is built along the crest of a ridge and although badly destroyed, the remains of square to oval house foundations are visible. The pottery did not look more Inca than that from some of the other villages such as Ichu. Interestingly, the foundations of what appeared to be Christian chapels were noted in two places. Cristobel Contochi, chief of Curamarka, also a *mitmaq* town, notes in his testimony in the *visita* of Iñigo Ortiz that they used to go to Warapa for baptism once a year.

Since our own brief work, Patrick Carmichael has done additional survey in *mitmaq* sites, and a report by him and Craig Morris is in press.[68] Suffice it to say here that they note a great deal of diversity among the *mitmaq* sites, but also record a tendency for there to be a higher proportion of Inca-inspired pottery than in the non-*mitmaq* villages, perhaps a reflection of their Cuzco origins or their closer ties with the state.

One of the most interesting of the *mitmaq* sites was that of Pachacoto. Unfortunately it, like the other *mitmaq* villages, was badly destroyed. Besides having a significant proportion of ceramics in the provincial Inca style of Huánuco Pampa, its locally made ceramics showed clear Cuzco influence. There was also a long rectangular building of the sort we have called *kallanka*. We believe these to be public buildings, and thus to indicate administrative or ceremonial importance for the sites that contain them.

The town of Warapa was the home of the main *mitmaq* leader by the time of the inspection of Iñigo Ortiz. The archaeological remains of Warapa lack public buildings from the Inca period, and in general have less evidence of relationships with Huánuco Pampa and the Inca. We suspect that the leadership position of the two settlements had been switched in the years following the European invasion. The possible Christian chapels in Warapa underscore a shift in public focus, but all our sources are silent on why such a shift might have occurred.

Many problems remain to be investigated. For example, did *mitmaq* colonists build their own houses or move into pre-existing villages vacated by the local people? If the latter, what modifications, if any, did they make? On the basis of the variety of ceramic styles, it appears that each *mitmaq* community made its own pottery rather than rely on local sources. How did the Inca provide for this? Did each *mitmaq* community have its own clay resources? The whole *mitmaq* picture, in short, remains somewhat unclear archaeologically.

In conclusion, we would reiterate the point we have been making throughout. Far from being a uniform state, the Inca empire was one of diversity, at least in this part of the realm, and we except, everywhere else. What would have happened had Francisco Pizarro not arrived as soon as he did we cannot say, but at the time of the Spanish Conquest Huánuco was made up of a great diversity of people living in different kinds of villages. About the only thing they had in common was a preference for locating their communities on the crests of ridges. This choice may have been dictated by practical reasons such as defense and/or preserving the best agricultural land from encroachment. Or, for all we know, aesthetics may also have played a part. There are few locations more dramatic than an Andean ridge crest with its awe-inspiring views of the surrounding landscape. The villages moreover were really integrated into that landscape in just the way that the architect Frank Lloyd Wright in a very different setting integrated his buildings with the midwestern prairies of North America.

10 Indirect rule and the ceremonies of state

Our story of Inca rule in Huánuco remains incomplete. Additional surveys and excavations are needed to give us a more complete perspective on both the local populations and the installations built by the state. We can, however, begin to sketch the outlines of Inca government in this one province of the empire. We can see how the state fulfilled its goals of conquest and acquired the resources to maintain itself, and how the state's activities affected the lives of the Chupaychu and other local peoples.

The Inca appear to have employed two principal means for controlling the region. One was carried out through the system of state settlements and roads. The other was carried out through local leaders in the incorporated polities. In some cases certain additional changes were made in the organization of the people in the countryside to render them more compliant and to bring them into conformity with administrative categories.

Our studies of the village sites emphasize the theme of ethnic diversity in the Huánuco area. In ceramics and in architecture, the Chupaychu, the Yacha and the Wamali are different from each other, and all three are collectively very distinct from the Inca. In a few instances there appears also to have been some internal variation within an ethnic group on the basis of the altitude and hence the principal economic activities of the individual community. Such a breakdown into a series of altitude-based economic subdivisions is a recognized Andean method for adding variety and safety to subsistence. The variations in temperature, rainfall, soils and altitude allowed different foods to be raised and provided security through diversity in ecological setting.

The fact that all three local groups shared a tendency to occupy highly defensible ridge crests serves to underline the hostility that existed between them, a situation also commented upon by the Spanish chronicler Cieza de León who reported of the Huánuco area that:

They tell that many of these tribes were brave and strong, and that before the Incas brought them under their rule many and cruel battles were fought between them, and that in most places the villages were scattered and so remote that there were no relations between them except when they met for their gatherings and feasts. On the hilltops they built their strong places and fortresses from which they made war on one another at the slightest pretext.[69]

On the other hand relationships within individual ethnic groups were apparently very strong, a suggestion given added weight by the persistence of such traditional relationships down to the present day. The Yacha of Cauri today trade for maize in Chaupiwaranga, a distant Yacha area in which they originally owned maize fields but no longer do so; on the other hand, they virtually ignore their nearby downstream neighbors who are former Wamali.

Most of the decisions that affected the daily lives of the local people undoubtedly remained at the local level, even those, such as marriages, that in theory were subject to review by the Inca. The operation of the historically known principle of indirect rule is reflected in the archaeology of Ichu, the Chupaychu capital. The Chupaychu chief lived in an elaborate house which combined Inca and Chupaychu architectural features: the rectangular shape and trapezoidal niches of the Inca and the square rooms with irregular niches of the Chupaychu. The status of the occupant was also expressed in the presence of Cuzco Polychrome-style pottery and evidence of a heavy entertainment schedule in the form of an active kitchen. Ichu, moreover, was deemed important enough to catch the attention of the Spaniards, who constructed a church there early in the post-Conquest period. All this contrasts markedly with the other remote villages we studied, which display only a few Inca ceramic traits as evidence of their subservience to the state.

The loss of autonomy by the local groups is not generally apparent in the architecture, which remained unaffected by changes in the economic and political spheres. Masonry techniques and spatial arrangements remained the same as in pre-Inca times until the villagers were relocated to Spanish-designed towns under the *reducción* policy of the 1570s.

Although the local groups gave up significant amounts of their time to till state fields, weave state cloth and fulfill other 'tax' obligations, they appear basically to have remained economically self-sufficient. We do not get the feeling by reading Iñigo Ortiz that the toppling of the Inca state by Spain had created local economic disruptions – except that the Spanish demands on the local economy were harsher than those of their predecessors.

Under Inca rule all local groups provided a part of their labor for the state, as is clearly documented in the *visita* of Iñigo Ortiz and the Espinoza Campos bridge investigation. The historical sources are largely reconfirmed in the archaeology. The presence of occasional Inca traits in the village pottery and of Inca storage facilities in a few of the villages speak to the degree – however superficial – to which the Inca permeated the local economy. Though remote from the major centers of political control the people were still required to do their part of the service to the state. This is reflected not only in the ethnohistorical evidence for *mit'a* service, but also in the physical evidence that local potters made ceramics for the state, some Inca traits thus becoming incorporated into the local ceramic tradition.

Against this background of continuity, self-sufficiency and indirect rule the Inca did make or were making a series of changes to strengthen administration, improve security and, perhaps, improve production in the state sector of the economy as well. For example, we know historically that for political and economic purposes the Inca moved segments of the population to different places as colonists, and we have located some of these known *mitmaq* sites in the Huánuco area. In addition, the enigmatic site of Aukimarka, which is reported as a Chupaychu village, suggests by its atypical architecture and ceramics that it does not belong in its entirety to the group to which it is ascribed, and may in fact represent either a *mitmaq* occupation which was not reported or some other kind of unrecorded reshuffling of the population in the Inca or possibly even the early Spanish Colonial period. Such unresolved questions emphasize some of the difficulties in making the fragmentary historical and archaeological records compatible with one another. At the same time they hint at a greater regrouping of people than we may realize.

The system of roads and settlements built by the Inca as a state intrusion into the local territory was certainly the most evident instrument of control. They modified both the settlement and socio-political landscape and introduced new elements of architectural and socio-political style. They also introduced a new level of governance. The primary purpose of the investigation at Huánuco Pampa and the state centers described in Chapters 4–7 was to explore the nature and effects of this new level of governance. The investigation took the form of trying to determine the patterns of activities in the sites during the final days of empire.

As we have seen, the architectural and ceramic remains suggest that the new level of governance was precisely that: a new level that remained separate from the existing polities of the region. The Inca policy in Huánuco appears to have emphasized the maintenance and manipulation of diversity rather than an attempt to integrate through the creation of cultural uniformity. We have seen the role of the centers along the road system as basically twofold. First, they provided an infrastructural network through which goods, information, and especially people could move. They physically tied the empire together. It is these functions of infrastructure that have been most stressed by previous studies, and in the smallest centers they were probably primary.

The second role of the centers was that of administration *per se*. How did the Inca from far off Cuzco acquire the political loyalty and economic support of the various polities of Huánuco? Our interpretation of the archaeological evidence, especially from Huánuco Pampa, does not see very much of the bureaucratic and military personnel we typically perceive as the controlling forces for far-flung empires. The emphasis instead is on feasting and ceremonies centered around the residence of the Inca or his representative. Elaborate architectural spaces were created which served as a backdrop for the ceremonial legitimizing of Inca rule. In city-like centers such as Huánuco Pampa local units were manipulated into a complicated and probably changing hierarchical order controlled from Cuzco.

The rules of the political algebra that made the growth of *Tawantinsuyu* possible will probably always remain somewhat elusive. Certainly we do not yet have enough information to detail them even for Huánuco. Warfare, both real and ritual, was certainly an element. The use of religion to legitimize authority was also important, and there are suggestions that a state ideology was involved. Economic factors were also central to the overall administrative strategy. On the one hand, the drinking, feasting and gift giving served to create bonds of reciprocity between rulers and ruled; on the other, resources were mobilized to support the various integrative mechanisms and the people who staffed them.

Some of the means of administration and control in Huánuco appear to have been quite fragile. Power that has to be constantly earned through reciprocity and legitimized through public display collapses when the devices that make the gifts and ceremonies possible are interrupted. The same principles that make it possible rapidly to manipulate existing units into quite large polities also makes those polities fragile – especially when extended to the scale of the Inca. The vulnerability of the Inca state to European invasion underscores this suggestion. The Inca strategy of moving populations about and making actual changes in the structure of the local populace was more permanent, but the evidence for its use in Huánuco is limited. In any case its ultimate effects would not necessarily have been to insure the endurance of any given hierarchical arrangement of the constituent polities, such as that dominated by the Inca.

We close by emphasizing once again an often-repeated theme. The hallmark of the Inca empire was its diversity. Thus the incomplete outline we have begun for the Inca rule of Huánuco cannot necessarily be applied to other regions of *Tawantinsuyu*. Dorothy Menzel pointed out the diverse patterns of Inca influence and control over several adjacent areas of the Peruvian south coast many years ago.[70] When we have information from the entire hinterland region that maintained contact with Huánuco Pampa we expect to see even more diversity within it than is apparent from the small part on which we have reported here. It is rather ironic that the great centers and monuments constructed by the Inca in similar styles in far-removed parts of the Andes have created the impression of a powerful, stable and relatively uniform state. When we narrow our focus to the actual operation of a specific region the picture changes to one of diversity and a system of government almost impossible to conceive of in terms designed for European nation states. The Inca political and economic achievement was based in large part on principles so dynamic they almost ensured that the state itself would be ephemeral.

Notes

Chapter 1

1 William H. Prescott, *History of the Conquest of Mexico and History of the Conquest of Peru*, The Modern Library, Random House, New York n.d., pp. 938–43. There is reason to doubt some of the details in this description on the basis of eyewitness accounts discovered since Prescott wrote.

2 Prescott, *op. cit.*, pp. 975–76.

3 John V. Murra, 'An Archaeological "Restudy" of an Andean Ethnohistorical Account', *American Antiquity*, 28 (1962a), pp. 1–4. Iñigo Ortiz de Zúñiga, *Visita de la Provincia de León de Huánuco en 1562, Tomo 1: Visita de las Cuatro Waranga de los Chupachu*, ed. John V. Murra, Universidad Nacional Hermilio Valdizán, Huánuco, Peru, 1967. Iñigo Ortiz de Zúñiga, *Visita de la Provincia de Leon de Huánuco en 1562, Tomo 2: Visita de los Yacha y Mitmagkuna Cuzqueños Encomendados en Juan Sanchez Falcón*, ed. John V. Murra, Universidad Nacional Hermilio Valdizán, Huánuco, Peru 1972.

Chapter 2

4 Rowe 1946, p. 185. Henry F. Dobyns and Paul L. Doughty, *Peru, Cultural History*, Oxford University Press, New York 1976, p. 61. Henry F. Dobyns, 'Estimating Aboriginal American Populations', *Current Anthropology*, 7 (4) (1966), Wenner-Gren Foundation for Anthropological Research, pp. 395–416, 425–49.

5 Some classic chronicles available in English would include Cieza de León 1959 [1553] and Garcilaso de La Vega 1966 [1604]. J. M. Cohen has provided a translation of Agustín de Zárate, *History of the Discovery and Conquest of the Province of Peru*, Penguin Books 1968 [1555], which is interwoven with selec-

tions from other chroniclers such as Francisco de Jeréz, Miguel de Estete and others. A number of older, somewhat inaccurate translations are to be found in the publications of the Hakluyt Society. For a facsimile edition of the only extensively illustrated manuscript on Inca and Colonial Peru see Felipe Guaman Poma de Ayala, *Nueva Coronica y Buen Gobierno*, Institut d'Ethnologie, Paris 1936 [1613]. A modern, annotated version is Felipe Guaman Poma de Ayala, *El primer Nueva Corónica y Buen Gobierno*, ed. John V. Murra and Rolena Adorno, Quechua transl. by Jorge L. Urioste, Siglo Vientiuno 1980. Major administration documents in addition to Ortiz 1967 and 1972, *op. cit.*, n. 3 above, would include Garci Diez de San Miguel, *Visita Hecha a la Provincia de Chucuito en el Año 1567*, Ediciones de la Casa de la Cultura, Lima, Peru 1964.

6 A reliable general account of the Inca remains Rowe 1946. The standard study of Inca economics is Murra 1980 [1955].

7 Roswith Hartmann 'Otros datos sobre las llamadas "Batallas Rituales"', *Actas y Memorias del XXXIX Congreso Internacional de Americanistas 6*, Lima 1977, pp. 125–35.

8 Louis Baudin, *A Socialist Empire: The Incas of Peru*, transl. Katherine Woods, ed. Arthur Goddard, Van Nostrand, Princeton 1961.

9 Catherine J. Julien, 'Inca Decimal Administration in the Laae Titicaca Region', in Collier *et al.* (eds.) 1982, pp. 119–51.

10 L. Leland Locke, *The Ancient Quipu or Peruvian Knot Record*, The American Museum of Natural History, New York 1923. Marcia Ascher and Robert Ascher, *Code of the Quipu, A Study in Media, Mathematics, and Culture*, University of Michigan Press, Ann Arbor 1981.

11 John V. Murra, 'El "Control Vertical" de un Máximo de Pisos Ecológicos en la Economía de las Sociedades Andinas', in Ortiz 1972, op.cit., n. 3 above, pp. 429–76.

12 John H. Rowe, 'The Origins of Creator Worship Among the Incas', in *Culture in History*, ed. Stanley Diamond, Columbia University Press 1960, pp. 408–29. Pease 1973. Arthur A. Demarest, *Viracocha, The Nature and Antiquity of the Andean High God*, Peabody Museum of Archaeology and Ethnology, Harvard University, Cambridge 1981.

13 Donald E. Thompson, 'Peasant Inca Villages in the Huánuco Region', *Verhandlungen des XXXVIII Internationalen Americanisten Kongresses, Stuttgart-München, 1968*, 4, Klaus Renner, Munich 1972, pp. 61–66. Donald E. Thompson, 'An Archaeological Evaluation of Ethnohistoric Evidence on Inca Culture', in *Anthropological Archaeology in the Americas*, ed. Betty Meggers, The Anthropological Society of Washington, Washington, D.C. 1968a, pp. 108–20. And Thompson 1968b.

Chapter 3

14 Cieza de León 1959, p. xli.

15 Cieza de León 1959, p. 110.

16 Guaman Poma de Ayala 1980, op. cit., n. 5 above, p. 185 [187].

17 Juan de Mori and Hernando Alonso Malpartida, 'La visitación de los pueblos chupachu, 1549', in Ortiz 1967, op. cit., n. 3 above, p. 297.

18 John V. Murra, 'La visita de los Chupaychu como fuente etnológica', in Ortiz 1967, op. cit., n. 3 above, p. 394.

19 Ortiz 1967, op. cit., n. 3 above, p. 41.

20 Ortiz 1967, op. cit., n. 3 above. p. 45.

21 Ortiz 1967, op. cit., n. 3 above, p. 71.

22 Ortiz 1972, op. cit., n. 3 above, pp. 80–81.

23 John V. Murra, 'El "Control Vertical" de un máximo de pisos ecológicos en la economía de las sociedades andinas', in Ortiz 1972, op. cit., n. 3 above, pp. 429–76.

24 Ortiz 1972, op. cit., n. 3 above, p. 227.

Chapter 4

25 Craig Morris, 'The Spanish Occupation of an Inca Administrative City', *Actes du XLII Congres International des Americanistes* IX-B, Paris 1980, pp. 209–19.

26 Gasparini and Margolies 1980.

27 John H. Rowe, *An Introduction to the Archaeology of Cuzco*, Papers of the Peabody Museum of American Archaeology and Ethnology 27 (2), Harvard University, Cambridge, Mass. 1944, p. 44.

28 Cristóbal de Molina ('el almagrista'), 'Destrucción del Perú', in *Las crónicas de los Molinas, Los Pegueños Grandes Libros de Historia Americana*, Ser. 1, Tomo IV, Lima 1943 [1553], p. 22. See also R. Tom Zuidema, 'El Ushnu', *Revista de la Universidad Complutense* 28 (117), Universidad Complutence, Madrid 1980, pp. 317–61, and Gasparini and Margolies 1980, pp. 264–80.

29 Rowe 1944, op. cit., n. 27 above, p. 24.

30 Rowe 1944, op. cit., n. 27 above, p. 24. Gasparini and Margolies 1980, pp. 181–94.

31 Craig Morris, 'Reconstructing Patterns of Non-Agricultural Production in the Inca Economy: Archaeology and Documents in Institutional Analysis', in *The Reconstruction of Complex Societies: An Archaeological Symposium*, ed. Charlotte Moore, The American Schools of Oriental Research, Cambridge, Mass. 1974, pp. 49–60. Craig Morris, 'Maize Beer in the Economics, Politics, and Religion of the Inka Empire', in *Fermented Food Beverages in Nutrition*, ed. Clifford F. Gastineau, William J. Darby, and Thomas B. Turner, The Nutrition Foundation, Academic Press, New York 1979, pp. 21–34.

32 In John H. Rowe, 'An Account of the Shrines of Ancient Cuzco', *Ñawpa Pacha* 17, Berkeley 1979, pp. 2–80.

33 Zuidema 1964. Nathan Wachtel, 'Estructuralismo e historia: a propósito de la organización social del Cuzco', in *Sociedad e ideología*, Instituto de Estudios Peruanos, Lima 1973, pp. 71–94.

34 Craig Morris, 'Architecture and the

Structure of Space at Huánuco Pampa', in *Tecnología, urbanismo, y arquitectura de los Incas*, ed. Graciano Gasparini and Luise Margolies, Ediciones Venezolanas de Antropología, Caracas (in press).

35 Craig Morris, 'The Identification of Function in Inca Architecture and Ceramics', *Revista del Museo Nacional* 37, Lima 1974, pp. 135–44.

Chapter 5

36 Murra 1980.

37 Craig Morris, 'The Infrastructure of Inka Control in the Peruvian Central Highlands', in Collier *et. al.* (eds.) 1982, pp. 153–71.

38 Gasparini and Margolies 1980, pp. 195–303.

39 Antonio Vásquez de Espinoza, *Compendio y descripción de las indias occidentales*, *Biblioteca de Autores Españoles*, 231, Atlas, Madrid 1969 [1628], p. 329.

40 John V. Murra, 'Cloth and Its Functions in the Inca State', *American Anthropologist* 64 (4) (1962), pp. 710–28.

41 Cieza de León 1959.

Chapter 6

42 Ortiz 1967, *op. cit.*, n. 3 above, pp. 25–26.

43 Cieza de León 1959, pp. 68–69.

44 Pedro Sancho, 'Relación para S. M. de lo sucedido en la conquista', *Colección de Libros y Documentos Referentes a la Historia del Perú* 1a serie, tomo 5, ed. Horacio H. Urteaga and Carlos A. Romero, Sanmartí, Lima 1917, pp. 194–95.

45 Garcilaso de la Vega 1966, pp. 241–42, 275, 395.

46 Carl Troll, *Las Culturas Superiores Andinas y el Medio Geografico*, transl. Carlos Nicholson, Publicaciones del Instituto de Geografía, Universidad Nacional Mayor de San Marcos, Lima pp. 34–35, Laminas III–VII.

47 Craig Morris, 'Tecnología y organización inca del almacenamiento de viveres en la sierra', *La Tecnología en el Mundo Andino* I, ed. Heather Lechtman

and Ana Maria Soldi, Universidad Nacional Autonima de Mexico, Mexico 1918, pp. 339–51.

48 Murra 1980, pp. 120–37.

49 Karl Polanyi, 'Marketless Trading in Hammurabi's Time', and 'The Economy as Instituted Process', in *Trade and Market in the Early Empires*, ed. Karl Polanyi, Conrad Arensberg, and Harry Pearson, The Free Press, Glencoe, Ill. 1957, pp. 12–26 and 243–70.

50 John V. Murra, 'Rite and Crop in the Inca State', in *Culture in History*, ed. Stanley Diamond, Columbia University Press, New York 1960, pp. 393–407.

Chapter 7

51 Donald E. Thompson and John V. Murra, 'The Inca Bridges in the Huánuco Region', *American Antiquity* 31 (5) (1966), pp. 632–39. Hyslop 1984.

52 Miguel de Estete, 'La relación del Viaje que hizo el Senor Hernando Pizarro . . . desde el Pueblo de Caxamalca a Parcama y de alli a Xauxa', in *Verdadera Relación de la Conquista del Perú y Provincia del Cuzco, Llamada Nueva Castilla* by Francisco de Xeréz, *Biblioteca de Autores Españoles* 26, Madrid 1853 [1534], p. 342.

53 Thompson and Murra 1966, *op. cit.*, n. 51 above.

54 The most complete source is Craig Morris, 'El Tampu Real de Tunsucancha', *Cuadernos de Investigación*, Universidad Nacional Hermilio Valdizán, Huánuco, Peru 1966. See also Hyslop 1984 and Thompson 1968b.

55 Hyslop 1984.

56 Thompson 1968b.

57 Hyslop 1984.

58 For a more complete discussion of the Bridge of Huánuco Viejo see Thompson and Murra 1966, *op. cit.*, n. 51 above.

59 Diego de Espinoza Campos, 'Los Indios del Repartimiento de Ichochuánuco contra Los Indios Pachas, sobre el Servicio y Mitas del Puente del Río Huánuco. Los Reyes, Febrero 9 de 1592', in Rolando Mellafe, 'La Significación Histórica de los Puentes en el Virreinato Peruano del Siglo XVI,' *Historio y Cultura* 1 (1), Lima

1965, p. 103. Translation in Thompson and Murra 1966, *op. cit.*, n. 51.

60 Taparaku is briefly discussed in Thompson and Murra 1966, *op. cit.*, n. 51.

Chapter 8

61 The figures and names in the following discussion are all drawn from Ortiz 1967, *op. cit.*, n. 3 above, *passim*. This publication also includes the Visita of 1549 among other supplementary documents. There are earlier publications of both *visitas*. Some discussion of the archaeological notes is also included in Donald E. Thompson, '*Investigaciones Arqueológicos en las Aldeas Chupachu de Ichu y Auguimarca*', in Ortiz 1967, *op. cit.*, n. 3 above, pp. 357–62; also Thompson 1968a, 1968b and 1972 *op. cit.*, n. 13 above.

62 See also Craig Morris, 'El Almacenaje en dos Aldeas de los Chupaychu', in Ortiz 1972, *op. cit.*, n. 3 above, pp. 383–404.

Chapter 9

63 Ortiz 1972, *op. cit.*, n. 3 above. Thompson 1967, *op. cit.*, n. 61 above, and 1968a, 1968b, 1972, *op. cit.*, n. 13 above.

64 Cezar Fonseca Martel, 'La Comunidad de Cauri y la Quebrada de Chaupi Waranga', *Cauadernos de Investicación* 1, Universidad Nacional Hermilio Valdizán, Huánuco, Peru 1966. Cezar Fonseca Martel, 'La Economía "Vertical" y la Economía de Mercado en las Comunidades Alteñas del Perú', in Ortiz 1972, *op. cit.*, n. 3 above, pp. 315–37.

65 Enrique Mayer, 'Censos insensatos: evaluación de los censos campesinos en la

historia de Tangor', in Ortiz 1972, *op. cit.*, n. 3 above, pp. 339–65.

66 In addition to our own observations, the following discussion draws heavily on Ramiro Matos, 'Wakan y Wamali: estudio arqueológico de dos aldeas rurales', in Ortiz 1972, *op. cit.*, n. 3 above, pp. 367–82.

67 Wamali sites have been described by Bertrand Flornoy, 'Exploration archeologique de l'Alto Marañón (des sources du Marañón au rio Sarma)', *Travaux* 5, Institut Français d'Etudes Andines, Lima-Paris 1955. See also Donald E. Thompson, 'Late Prehistoric Occupations in the Eastern Peruvian Andes', *Revista del Museo Nacional* 37, Lima 1971, pp. 116–23. Donald E. Thompson, 'Buildings are for People: Speculations on the Aesthetics and Cultural Impact of Structures and their Arrangement', *Prehistoric Settlement Patterns: Essays in Honor of Gordon R. Willey*, University of New Mexico Press and Harvard University, Cambridge, Mass. 1983, pp. 115–27.

68 Patrick Carmichael and Craig Morris, 'The Mitmaq of Huánuco: An Archaeological Survey of Graves Resettled by the Inca and Recorded in 1562 Inspection of Iñigo Ortiz de Zúñiga'. Manuscript to be published in the *Anthropological Papers of the American Museum of Natural History*, New York.

Chapter 10

69 Cieza de Leòn 1959, p. 109.

70 Dorothy Menzel, 'The Inca occupation of the south coast of Peru', *Southwestern Journal of Anthropology* 15 (1959), pp. 125–42.

Select bibliography

CIEZA DE LEON, Pedro *The Incas*, transl. Harriet de Onis, ed. Victor von Hagen, University of Oklahoma Press, Norman 1959.

COLLIER, George, ROSALDO, Renato I. and WIRTH, John D. (eds.) *The Inca and Aztec States 1400–1800: Anthropology and History*, Academic Press, New York 1982.

GARCILASO DE LA VEGA ('El Inca') *Royal commentaries of the Incas and General History of Peru*, transl. Harold V. Livermore, Austin and London 1966.

GASPARINI, Graciano and MARGOLIES, Luise *Inca Architecture*, transl. Patricia J. Lyon, Indiana University Press, Bloomington 1980.

HEMMING, John *The Conquest of the Incas*, Macmillan, London and Harcourt, Brace, Jovanovich, New York 1970 (Penguin paperback 1983).

HYSLOP, John *The Inca Road System*, Academic Press, New York 1984.

LUMBRERAS, Luis G. *The Peoples and Cultures of Ancient Peru*, transl. Billy J. Meggars, Smithsonian Institution Press, Washington 1974.

MÉTRAUX, Alfred *The History of the Incas*, Schocken Books, New York 1970.

MORRIS, Craig 'State Settlements in Tawantinsuyu: A Strategy of Compulsory Urbanism', in *Contemporary Archaeology*, ed. Mark Leone, Southern Illinois University Press, Carbondale 1972, pp. 393–401.

MURRA, John V. *Formaciones Economicas y Politicos del Mundo Andino*, Instituto de Estudios Peruanos, Lima 1975.

—— *The Economic Organization of the Inca State*, JAI Press, Greenwich, Conn. 1980 [1955].

PEASE, Franklin G.Y. *El Dios Creador Andino*, Mosca Azul, Lima 1973.

PRESCOTT, William H. *History of the Conquest of Mexico and History of the Conquest of Peru*, The Modern Library, Random House, New York n.d. (originally published in 1847).

ROSTWOROWSKI DE DIEZ CANSECO, Maria *Etnia y Sociedad*, Instituto de Estudios Peruanos, Lima 1977.

ROWE, John H. 'Inca Culture at the time of the Spanish conquest', in *Handbook of South American Indians*, 2, ed. Julian H. Steward, Smithsonian Institution, Bulletin 143, Washington 1946, pp. 183–330.

SQUIER, George E. *Peru: Incidents of Travel and Exploration in the Land of the Incas*, Harper and Brothers, New York 1877.

THOMPSON, Donald E. 'Huánuco, Peru: A Survey of a Province of the Inca Empire', *Archaeology*, 21 (3) (1968), pp. 174–81.

WACHTEL, Natan *Sociedad e Ideología*, Instituto de Estudios Peruanos, Lima 1973.

ZÁRATE, Agustín de *et al. History of the Discovery and Conquest of Peru*, transl. J.M. Cohen, Penguin Books, Harmondsworth 1968.

ZUIDEMA, R. Tom *The Ceque System of Cuzco, The Social Organisation of the Capital of the Inca*, International Archives of Ethnography, supplement to vol. I, E.J. Brill, Leiden 1964.

Acknowledgments

First and foremost we acknowledge the great debt to John V. Murra. The idea to study the Huánuco region was his; the realization of the anthropological importance of the *visita* of Iñigo Ortiz was his; the project that conducted the original research was directed by him. Furthermore, he has been a constant champion of the need to coordinate archaeological and historical studies – particularly in research on the Inca. During the years of Morris' Huánuco Pampa project his input continued to play a strong role in the research.

It is not possible to acknowledge the contributions of all the more than 300 people who have been associated with the research in its various phases and aspects. However, it is necessary to single out Delfin Zúñiga of Yaca and Huánuco. He began with us on the initial survey in 1964. For the later research in the city he undertook assignments ranging from logistics manager, through topographic and drafting work, to substantial amounts of computer work. Others who made notable contributions during the research were: Ramiro Matos, Robert Bird, Cezar Fonseca, Peter Jenson, Santiago Japa, the late Emilio Mendizabal, Dan Shea, Pat Stein, William Burke, Idilio Santillana, Freddy Ferrua, Carlos Meneses, Patricia Netherly, James Donegan, Hugo Ludeña, Oscar Paredes, Juan Carbojal, Cesar Durand, Judith Cardich, Corine Varon, Aldo Bolaños, Juan Raimerez, Manuel Calderon, Maria Dianderas, Elizabeth Wing, Elizabeth Reitz, Denise Pozzi, Carmen Cardoza, Cay Loria and Peter Kvietok.

John Hyslop and Patricia Bramwell made invaluable contributions to the manuscript and Nicholas Amorosi to the artwork.

The major financial support for the work came from the National Science Foundation. It began with a grant to John Murra, through the Institute of Andean Research, sponsor of the original project. There was a grant to Thompson for data analysis and, in the 1970s, a series of grants to Morris for Huánuco Pampa. Additional support was provided by the Graduate School Research Committee and the Ibero-American Studies Program of the University of Wisconsin and by the American Museum of Natural History.

List of illustrations

Unless otherwise credited, photographs are by Craig Morris or Donald E. Thompson.

Color plates

Monochrome plates

Figures

Index

Figure numbers appear in **bold** and plate numbers in *italic*